Israel and the Politics of Jewish Identity _____

Israel and the Politics of Jewish Identity

The Secular-Religious Impasse

Asher Cohen and Bernard Susser

The Johns Hopkins University Press | *Baltimore and London*

© 2000 The Johns Hopkins University Press
All rights reserved. Published 2000
Printed in the United States of America on acid-free paper
9 8 7 6 5 4 3 2 1

The Johns Hopkins University Press
2715 North Charles Street
Baltimore, Maryland 21218-4363
www.press.jhu.edu

Library of Congress Cataloging-in-Publication Data will
be found at the end of this book.
A catalog record for this book is available from the
British Library.

ISBN 0-8018-6345-7

To my wife, Liora, and my children,
Avia, Mody, and Elia with love

To the Pearls and the Mother of Pearls:
Susan, Shellie, Donna—who make me a very lucky man

Contents

This book got its start in heated, often combative, conversations between the coauthors. Both of us were deeply anxious about the conflict between the secular and religious communities and the direction it
was taking in the Jewish state of Israel. Much of what follows reflects
our common fear that the deteriorating relations between the secular and
religious communities in Israel may be approaching a point of no return.

Our study attempts to be dispassionate and fair minded, but we make
no claims for objectivity. We are, to be sure, academic students of the
subject, but we are also committed partisans in the struggle—a struggle
that is taking place as these very words are being written. We write in
medias res, with new developments tripping over one another in furious
succession. This is said at the very outset to declare our overriding interest: we are deeply concerned that secular-religious conflict, as it has developed over the past two decades, threatens the integrality of the Jewish state.

Although we resigned ourselves early on to the futility of attempting
to write an objective book, there is, nevertheless, a built-in mechanism
that has made it hard for partisan arguments to seep into the text, a
mechanism that has kept us both honest. One of the authors is American born, leads a more or less secular life, is an outspoken dove with
sympathies for the Meretz Party and the left wing of the Labor Party,
and voted for Ehud Barak in the 1999 elections. The other author is
Israeli born, wears a knitted *kipah*, leads a religious life, is a hawk in
political ideology, voted for Benjamin Netanyahu and the National Religious Party, and is not at all pleased with the Oslo Peace Accords. This,
we realize, does not guarantee objectivity, but it does encourage a kind
of impartiality. We could not help but guard against our own tendencies
to write as we wished. We both felt compelled to avoid the kind of po-
lemical tone that compromises balance and fairness. When such partisan tones were inadvertently introduced, one or the other of us objected,
and the offending passage was removed. The aim was always to achieve
a degree of dispassion that would render the argument acceptable to
both of us. The text before you is, therefore, not so much a compromise

(although there were compromises here and there) as an attempt at an impartial analysis that has passed the critical evaluation of two individuals who belong to the opposite camps of the very struggle they seek to understand.

Research for this book took us beyond the standard and rather voluminous literature on religion and state in Israel. Much of what we recount and analyze relates to developments that were happening around us as we wrote—hence, the large number of newspaper reports, speeches, and debates we cite. Arbitrarily (but inevitably), we were compelled to agree on a cut-off date beyond which we would not include new material. The book is updated until and including the May 1999 elections. It discusses, in a preliminary way, Ehud Barak's negotiations to form a new coalition government. It should be noted, as well, that our study is distinctive in that it is largely based on Hebrew primary sources.

We also depart from the familiar "religion and state" framework because we believe it to be anachronistic. The only frame large enough to contain the struggle as it is shaping up today is what we speak of as the politics of Jewish identity, which is another way of saying that the relatively circumscribed battle over whether this or that religious practice would be officially adopted has given way to a principled and broad-based struggle over the very identity of the Jewish collectivity in Israel.

It is our fervent hope that the following analysis will make some small contribution toward recognizing the potential danger involved in the clash. Understanding the nature of the confrontation is, after all, the first step toward defusing it.

Prologue

From Compromise to Crisis

At midday on Friday the fifth day of Iyyar, Tashach (14 May 1948), with the Sabbath quickly approaching, Israel's Declaration of Independence was being drafted by a senior assembly of jurists and politicians. Their progress was stymied by a thorny dilemma: should the declaration make reference to the "God of Israel"? For the religious participants, it was simply unthinkable that thanks not be given to the Holy One, Blessed Be He in this unparalleled moment, when Jewish sovereignty in the Land of Israel was being renewed after two millennia of exile. For the secular, many of whom were radical Marxists and militant freethinkers, the very mention of God was an affront to their most cherished beliefs. A seemingly insurmountable dilemma at a most inopportune time! Were the discussions to drag on into the Sabbath, even if some satisfactory solution could be reached, the Jewish state would be "born in sin," that is, in violation of the Sabbath. For the religious, this was an appalling prospect.

Deliverance came in the form of a cleverly ambiguous formula with which both sides could live. It declared that Israel's independence was born "out of *betachon* in the Rock of Israel" (*metoch betachon be'Zur Yisrael*).[1] The phrase was doubly equivocal. First, the term *betachon* could mean either "security," as in military security, or "faith," as in faith in the Lord. Moreover, whereas the religious understood "Rock of Israel" as a simple reference to the Divine, the secular could interpret it in its more poetic sense, connoting Jewish resolve and perpetuity.

An attempt by Mapam, a radical left-wing party, to have Israel's independence declared at midnight, when the mandate formally expired, was rejected out of hand because of its transparently antireligious motives. In the end, when the declaration was completed, it had the support of a remarkably broad coalition of signatories, ranging from the fundamentalist Agudat Israel Party to the Israeli Communist Party. After the signatures were affixed, Rabbi Maimon, the representative of the Mizrahi Party, intoned the blessing, thanking God for having allowed "us to live and see this day" *(shehechianu)*, while David Ben-Gurion listened bareheaded.[2] Here then, at the very moment of Israel's inception, we find the kinds of concessions, compromises, deference, and creative ambiguities to which we refer as *consociational politics*.

Nearly fifty years later, in the summer of 1997, a notice publicized in the media called on Israelis to participate in a public demonstration aimed at stopping the Haredim (ultra-Orthodox). The bluntness of the call created a public outcry.[3] The demonstration's organizers accused the Haredim of inflaming the already charged relations between the secular and religious in Israel by insisting that yeshiva students in growing numbers be exempt from military service and by exploiting their pivotal position in the Knesset to press an agenda of religious coercion. Dominique Bourel, head of the French Institute for the Study of Israel, has described the prevailing atmosphere as follows: "It seems to me that secular-religious coexistence has given way to secular fanaticism and religious fanaticism. . . . I have many Israeli friends in academia, and I am shocked anew each time by the power of the hatred they hold for the ultra-Orthodox."[4] The ultra-Orthodox did not forbear. They retaliated with slogans such as "the Fourth Reich" and "Isra-Nazis."

A few months later, a group calling itself Secular Jewish Faith (Emunah Chilonit Yehudit) took out full-page ads in Israel's newspapers that called for "repentance" from the ritualistic, halachic, doctrinaire religious direction the country was taking. Comparing the surge of Israeli religiosity to that of Iran, Algeria, and Afghanistan, they warned that the handwriting was already on the wall. What, they asked rhetorically, if the forces of this religiosity should triumph and liberal democracy be routed? Then "we will surrender and retreat quietly to the Diaspora to await true Jewish deliverance . . . in which freedom of thought is a more important value than the length of one's *tzitziot* [ritual fringes]."

At the close of 1997, another broad-based advertising campaign was launched. One newspaper ad warned, "When your son invites you to 'make Shabbat' with him in Bnei Brak [an ultra-Orthodox city] it will already be too late."[5] The ad spoke with alarm of Israel's *hitchardut* (the growing dominance of the Haredim), which "threatens each and every one of us." It closed with the demand that the secular majority be appropriately represented—in other words, that it be as overwhelming in influence and power as it was overwhelming in numbers.

Separated by nearly a half century, these events exemplify the thesis that underlies this study: secular-religious relations have gone from compromise to crisis, from mitigating arrangements to aggravated strife, from bad to worse. Consociationalism—that is, the adaptive, unity-preserving political style of the first decades of Israel's existence—has given way, especially in the past decade and a half, to a crisis-dominated relationship between secular and religious Jews that becomes progressively more strident as the erstwhile common political language between them is lost. Rather than an accommodation of each other's needs in the interest of preserving national unity, a majoritarian, winner-take-all style has grown more and more dominant.

Exacerbating this deteriorating relationship and severely complicating the prognosis for the future are two concurrent but antithetical processes that are visibly transforming Israeli public and private life. On the one hand, it is impossible to miss the growing Westernization of Israeli life. Styles of consumption, leisure, and travel, the dominance of multinational corporations and marketing chains, cosmopolitan media exposures, computer technology and communication, and, of course, growing affluence are bringing Israel closer and closer to the American and Western European standard. Doubtless, this will bring great pressure to bear on traditional prohibitions and commandments (the burgeoning of nonkosher restaurants is only one example) that do not easily accommodate themselves to contemporary Western life patterns.

At the same time, the political power of the religious, particularly the Haredim, is growing apace. Because of their demographic fecundity and the increasing legitimacy and pervasiveness of their agenda, they represent a growing proportion of Israel's electorate. Moreover, they have succeeded in amassing support among non-Haredi populations—particularly among traditional Sephardi voters. Buoyed by their successes and increasingly confident of their power, Haredi politics has become aggressive and contentious. No longer are the Haredim content to concern themselves with their own communal needs, as was predominantly the case during the early years of statehood; presently, they are skilled political protagonists who ardently advocate assertive and articulate policies in security issues and foreign affairs, in national economic policy, and, of course, in defending and promoting Israel's religious character.

All this, of course, is not to say that Israel lacked secular-religious crises in the first decades of statehood or, for that matter, that there are no areas of compromise and accommodation at present. Indeed, for those familiar with the historical record, many of the current crises have a distinctly déjà vu quality to them. Much of the current secular-religious debate is a throwback to previous decades: there is, for example, nothing new under the sun in their reciprocal name-calling. For secular militants, the religious were and remain the forces of darkness and superstition; for religious radicals, the secular conduct inquisitions and pogroms against anything that smacks of Jewish tradition. The violent struggles over Sabbath traffic on Jerusalem's Bar-Ilan Street in 1996–97 recall similar struggles in the 1980s in the Ramot neighborhood and earlier, in the 1950s, in Sabbath Square and at the Mandelbaum Gate. The "Who Is a Jew?" debate of the 1950s and 1960s is currently reenacted in the form of the controversial 1997 Chok Ha'hamara (Conversion Law). From the status quo to religious coercion to a halachic state, the old commonplaces seem to live on, indeed, to flourish. Many observers of Israel's religio-political life do, in fact, contend that little is really novel in today's religio-political strife.[6]

It is our contention that similarities to the past notwithstanding, the secular-religious cleft in Israeli society today finds itself in a new and especially perilous phase. We are witnessing not merely an extrapolation of past animosities into present-day realities but rather important changes in the character, context, and dramatis personae of the religio-secular confrontation. It is tempting to say that this fateful encounter remains much like the past, only more so—more intense, more fraught, more spiteful; but to do so would be to overlook how successive cumulative changes can alter the very nature of a conflict. Essentially, the transformation of recent years can be summed up as follows: No longer do secular and religious Jews attempt to mediate their differences and moderate potential conflicts through an elaborate system of concessions, mutual deference, and demarcated spheres of autonomy. They are, at present, both playing to win.

Israel and the Politics of Jewish Identity _____

Chapter One

Religion and State in Israel
A Historical and Conceptual Framework

This opening chapter addresses two central issues. First, we survey the major events and developments that have historically influenced the relationship of religion to state in Israel. Second, we explore the nature of consociationalist democracy, focusing especially on its characteristic principles and patterns of behavior and on the sociopolitical conditions that encourage its adoption and application.

Historical Origins

Secularism as a worldview was virtually unknown before the European Enlightenment of the eighteenth century. Although the Jewish Enlightenment, or Haskalah, tarried somewhat behind its European counterpart, it too, in its turn, challenged the traditional credos and dominant behavior patterns of the Jewish status quo ante. Before the Haskalah, Judaism's theocentric axioms together with its attendant traditions constituted the unchallenged and exclusive regulators of collective, individual, and institutional life.

The transition to modernity in the West typically entailed a dramatic shift to anthropocentric assumptions, that is, to the conviction that societies as well as individuals choose, even construct, their values, cultures, and beliefs.[1] If they can be chosen and constructed thus, they could have been chosen and constructed otherwise. Beliefs and practices, therefore, are not cosmic givens, as the traditionalists insisted; rather, they must be consciously taken, that is, adopted, by human beings.[2] In such a world, tradition is "decentered" and "demythologized." It becomes merely one option among many: vulnerable to critique, open to revision, even liable to root-and-branch rejection.[3]

Were we to draw up an overall balance sheet of the modernity-traditionalism struggle over the past three centuries, there can be little doubt that modernity has emerged the victor. This is especially true in the Jewish context.[4] If, in the year 1700, nontraditional Jews were a bizarre rarity, some three hundred years later they account for the lion's share of world Jewry. Even in Israel—which is probably the most traditional of all major Jewish concentrations in the world—some 80 percent of the population cannot be characterized as observant and Orthodox in the traditional manner. Even among those who define themselves as Orthodox and observant, a substantial majority are "modern" in dress, occupation, and lifestyle. It is not too much to say that Jews have undergone more radical transformations in belief and practice during the last two and a half centuries than in the millennium and a half that preceded them. Nor can it be doubted that the advent of modernity has posed the most vexing and unmanageable challenge to the Jewish religious tradition in all of Jewish history.[5]

Virtually every major creed that has emerged within the Jewish community over the past two centuries—whether religious or secular in character—derives in one way or another from this confrontation between traditionalism and modernity.[6] Indeed, what currently divides Jewish allegiances most essentially is the position they occupy between the poles of the traditionalist status quo ante and Western modernity. At the most basic level, Jews confronting the challenge of the Haskalah needed to choose between social isolation and religious conservatism, on the one side, and adjustment and Westernization, on the other. This primary decision compelled a secondary, more finely tuned practical choice. Isolation, like Westernization, lacks specificity: both are compatible with a great variety of different practices. Just as Westernization can take many forms, some retaining substantial traditional elements, so isolation is rarely complete.[7] How this fine-tuning played itself out in the Jewish ideological controversies of the twentieth century provides the background to our study of the politics of Jewish identity.

In what follows we narrow our focus and highlight the two reactions to modernity that figure most centrally in our analysis: the various forms of Orthodoxy and the Jewish national movement known as Zionism. It is in the internal developments of each and in their often stormy relations with each other that the politics of Jewish identity is played out in contemporary Israel.

Despite its claims to possess unbroken continuity with the Jewish past, Orthodox Judaism is a modern phenomenon. Both as a term and as a practice, Orthodoxy represents the conscious reaction of traditional Judaism to the challenge of Westernizing secularism.[8] No longer did the unconfronted Jewish tradition instinctively and mimetically recreate itself generation after generation; it now needed to deal with threatening alternatives that were cutting deep inroads into its most secure heartland.

Some of those called Orthodox reaffirmed their loyalty to what they understood to be the status quo ante: there would be no compromise with the heresy that called itself Enlightenment. Judaism had lived *alongside* rather than *within* Western civilization for centuries, and it must continue to preserve its distance and its holy isolation. For these "neo-traditionals,"[9] "novelty" (in the words of one of their leaders, the Chatam Sofer) "was prohibited by Torah injunction" *(chadash asur min Ha'torah)*. Hence, modernity needed to be repudiated altogether. Neo-traditional Orthodoxy adopted a sternly isolationist posture in its dealings with the non-Jewish world and a stance of unmitigated condemnation toward those Jews who collaborated with the enemy.

By contrast, those described as modern Orthodox adopted a more positive, accommodationist attitude toward the contemporary world.[10] Although they retained a resolute loyalty to Halacha (the body of Jewish scriptural law), isolation per se was not viewed as a virtue. Modernity, they would say, is not necessarily inimical to the religious life; properly pursued, it creates significant opportunities for religious self-realization. Whether through selective adjustments to Western culture, or by compartmentalizing life into religious and neutral zones, or, most ambitiously, through synthetic interpretations that compound modernity and tradition, the objective of modern Orthodoxy is to live authentically in both worlds simultaneously.

How these differing forms of Orthodoxy related to Jewish nationalism as an ideology and, above all, to the Jewish society that Zionism created in Palestine/Israel lies at the heart of our project. In the Eastern European heartland of traditional Orthodoxy, attempts to frustrate the widespread modernizing tendencies of the Maskilim (purveyors of enlightenment) met with only partial success, despite determined efforts by the traditional leadership. From the 1880s onward, however, the enemy changed identity and began to pose an even more nontraditional challenge. These new enemies were modernists, to be sure, but of a new and unprecedented stripe: they were Jewish nationalists, more commonly known as Zionists. Although a relatively small percentage of Zionists were religious, for the most part Zionism possessed powerfully modernizing and aggressively secularizing tendencies. As such, it earned the profound enmity of the traditional community. (One sage spoke of it as "the collective evil urge [yetzer harah] of the Jewish people"). Zionism was disdained, first of all, because the very susceptibility to nationalist themes reflected an openness to the nationalist currents that were sweeping non-Jewish Europe. Second, it was clear to the neotraditionalists that the essence of the Zionist "revolt" was a rejection of the Jewish status quo ante. Only those who were equivocal about religion as the binding element of Jewish unity were likely to look for an alternate or even a supplementary bond in national solidarity.

Indeed, many Zionists openly declared that Jewish nationalism was the modern surrogate for anachronistic religious loyalties. Religion, they asserted, was undeniably a part of the Jewish heritage, and yet in its traditional form, it was antiquated and corrupt. What could be transposed into the modern national idiom and made over into secular culture should be salvaged, and what was narrowly halachic and theological should be discarded.

Between the traditionalists and the secular Zionists stood the religious Zionists. Theirs was a complex and multifaceted stance. Being both Zionist and religious, they were simultaneously allies and enemies to both sides. They mediated between the poles and, like so many mediators, were often charged with treachery by both sides. The history of religious Zionism chronicles the shifting and intricate relationships, the strains and pressures, that resulted from the confrontation with its two polar allegiances.[11]

But friction between the religious and the secular was only one of many rich sources of conflict among the ideological and communal protagonists that populated the Jewish world.[12] Indeed, when a substantial Jewish contingent settled in Palestine in the first decades of the twentieth century, a riot of cleavage lines crisscrossed the diminutive community. There were controversies between the narrowly nationalist and the more cosmopolitan communities, socioeconomic splits between the socialists and the liberals, communal tensions between Ashkenazi and

Sephardi Jews, ideological struggles between Zionists and non-Zionists, political strife between activist hawks and pragmatic doves, and of course, religious contention between the traditional and the secular. What is most remarkable about the history of the Jewish national community in the prestate era—the Yishuv—is how it managed to retain its fragile unity despite these many profound schisms that rent its social fabric.

This accomplishment is all the more intriguing given that the Yishuv institutions were anything but sovereign or authoritative. They were, in the end, based upon voluntary membership and elective submission to the institutions' injunctions. For example, Yishuv institutions could not tax the Jewish population under its sway without their willing approval; neither could they punish recalcitrant groups and individuals unless these groups first accepted its authority. Moreover, in order for its decisions to be binding, Yishuv institutions required the legitimation of the many contentious factions out of which they were constituted—an often daunting task. How then did this embattled, fractured, and noncompulsory political community succeed in maintaining its integrity and authority over the course of a number of crisis-filled decades? How could such a ramshackle institutional structure not only successfully manage the Yishuv's affairs—at times with notable intergroup cooperation—but also be poised to create a sovereign Jewish state when the mandate drew to a close?

The widely accepted answer is that Yishuv institutions operated within a consociational context, that is, they were governed by patterns of mutual accommodation.[13] The common goal of achieving Jewish statehood and the urgent need for unity in the face of the hostile forces that threatened from without drove the constituent groups of the Yishuv to value institutional integrity above their own immediate interests. The recognition that "united we stand, divided we fall" induced the various groups to carefully guard the balance between the various contending communal interests. It was apparent that playing to win, although it might bring short-term gains, would spell catastrophe for the essential goals of the Yishuv as a whole. Hence, ideological and practical disputes needed to be suppressed, detoured, and defused. Through an elaborate network of compromises, concessions, and patterns of reciprocal deference, institutions that might otherwise have disintegrated through conflict retained their integrity—indeed, functioned with noteworthy political efficacy. Consociational arrangements deterred conflict along a broad front of issues; it is, in fact, broadly accepted that consociationalism governed virtually all aspects of the Yishuv's fractious communal life.

After the Jewish state came into being, this conflict-deterring style became largely anachronistic, gradually declining into obsolescence. After all, a sovereign state does not require communal unanimity to pursue its policies. Yet the residual idea that consensus is a high political virtue, that groups ought not be pushed to the point of dangerous alienation, that deals and arrangements are superior to one-sided victory, all of these persisted well after the founding of the state. Above all, however, the full consociational style endured in one particularly charged issue area: the religious-secular divide. In this explosive arena, the fear of unmanageable conflict over the very essence of Jewish identity in the Jewish state rendered the consociational style enduringly relevant, perhaps even mandatory.[14] Current surveys consistently report that the religious-secular cleavage is perceived by Israelis as the bitterest and most intractable of sociopolitical conflicts—almost twice as much so as the cleavage between doves and hawks. Even a cursory recounting of the disputes that have agitated Israeli public life in the five decades of the Jewish state's existence will immediately highlight the persistence, frequency, and incendiary nature of those conflicts. The sources of friction between these communities range over many areas of public and private life:

1. Differences of ideological principle over the relevance of Halacha for public policy and national identity are a constant source of discord.

2. The translation of these disputes into coalitional wrangles and budgetary infighting between religious and secular parties only aggravates these abrasive tendencies.

3. The legislative and quasi-constitutional battles to incorporate religious or secular worldviews into the country's formal legal structure are perhaps the most regular and predictable fixture in all of Israel's public life.

4. Finally, the social segregation of many religious groups from secular Israel (and vice versa) creates stubborn stereotypes and deep-seated belligerence.

Faced with such acute and perennial sources of conflict, it comes as no surprise that consociational patterns persisted here even when they waned elsewhere.

Consociational Democracy: Principles and Practice

The identification and description of consociationalism as a distinctive form of democratic political organization is largely the work of the Dutch political scientist Arend Lijphart. In a series of wide-ranging studies, Lijphart explains how consociationalism is adopted and practiced in polities where deep social and political cleavages threaten the institutions of public life with destabilization and delegitimation.[15] Consociational arrangements tend to thrive when the differences between a political system's constituent groups are so severe that allowing them to develop unchecked threatens to issue in unity-shattering crises, violent conflict, even the disintegration of the political community. Consociationalism is, then, a method of organizing intercommunal relations so as to mitigate the effects of conflict. When consociational patterns are prevalent, societies with severe ideological, religious, and ethnic divides can, nonetheless, conduct their business civilly and sensibly—without having the various groups grow any fonder of, or closer to, one another. In a word, consociationalism explains how deeply divided societies— societies we might otherwise think were politically doomed—can function reasonably well over long periods of time.

An important distinction between two levels of religious and cultural conflict needs to be drawn at the very outset. First, there is the broad national level in which struggles relate to the very identity and character of the state. At this level, issues take on principled and symbolic form. Each side aspires to stamp its own values and perspectives onto the identity of the political community. The second level, by contrast, is narrower and more concrete. It relates to the desire of every group to lead its life as it sees fit, with what it considers adequate levels of resources, dignity, and autonomy. It should be immediately clear that a narrow-gauged cleavage focusing on satisfactory allocations and functional autonomy is substantially less threatening to the well-being of the polity than one whose scope is general and whose objectives relate to the essential character of the political community.

Consociationalism attempts to orchestrate group relations at both these levels by establishing regulating principles that inhibit conflict and neutralize it when it does erupt. Clearly, the chances of success are greater when the conflict is narrow. We can flesh out the varied conflict-deflecting strategies in the consociational repertoire to great advantage

by briefly illustrating them in the context of religion and public life in
Israel.[16]

Refrain from Decisive Settlements in
Conflict-Ridden Issues

Decisive outcomes to political struggles normally mean that one side
has won and the other has lost. Decisive outcomes of this kind, especially when the struggle is over issues of cardinal importance, can be
intolerable for the loser. Indeed, the sense of loss can be so keen that the
defeated side suffers a basic crisis of confidence in the polity—leading to
its destabilization and delegitimation. Refraining from clear decisions
permits all the contending political camps to maintain their loyalty to
the political system, to view it as legitimate. Creative ambiguities, equivocal formulas, and simply leaving issues unresolved discourage radical
political currents from dominating. The state continues to be perceived
as a reasonably honest broker and impartial arbitrator rather than the
executor of the enemies' will. Although no one side gets all it wants—
militants will always clamor for crises and ultimatums—each side gets
enough to render councils of despair and strife unconvincing and unattractive.

Israel's lack of separation between religion and state is a way of avoiding the decisive resolution of a deeply contentious issue. Despite its character as a liberal Western state, Israel has adopted an intricate mosaic of
religious and secular policies and institutions that render it quite unique.
To be sure, the religious element in public life is much less pervasive than
what the traditional community would prefer, but it is also considerably
more so than what principled Israeli secularists would freely endorse.
Irresolution, adopting elusive formulas (such as maintenance of the status quo), and allocating sufficient resources to all parties preserve the
secular-religious divide in a state of negotiated balance that prevents a
potentially ruinous Kulturkampf from erupting.

Refrain from Utilizing Simple Majorities to Decide
Contentious Issues

Refraining from decisive resolution does not necessarily derive from
a balance of power between the contending camps. Although political
equilibrium between the various disputants may well encourage conso-

ciational arrangements, the consociational style is considerably more manifest when one side to the conflict could win handily by recruiting its numerical plurality—and yet chooses not to do so. The distinctiveness of consociationalism becomes apparent in such circumstances: despite numerical superiority and the seduction to parley its majority into political victory, the larger and powerful group resists the natural tendency to press its advantage. It desists from what would be easy victory and chooses instead to accommodate the minorities by negotiating compromise solutions.

The religious camp in Israel has always been a minority community, constituting roughly one-fifth of the population. During the period of dominance by the Mapai Party, it did not even possess the critical coalitional role it now enjoys. Mapai (the Israeli Workers' Party), together with its other mostly labor-socialist allies, enjoyed a decisive and uncontested majority. In such circumstances it would have been only natural for this powerful and ideologically ardent camp to reject religious demands—especially those going beyond communal autonomy, those aimed at the very character of the state itself. Yet they consistently chose to avoid inflaming the religious-secular cleavage, opting instead for compromise, deference, and accommodation.

Recognize the "Red Lines" (Tolerance Limits) of the Other Side and Its Right of Veto in Such Matters

Every political camp has its limits, the point beyond which compromise is no longer an option. The consociational style encourages each of the clashing sides to identify the other community's "red lines," their tolerance limits, and to respect their right to disqualify egregiously offending measures. Each side makes clear what transgresses its most deeply held values, what constitutes an unbearable affront to its way of life. What is more, each side expects these sensitivities to be respected by the other political players.

In the lengthy and fraught relations between the secular and the religious communities in Israel, these "red lines" have often been closely approached. Yet in a wide variety of issues, ranging from the exemption of religious women and yeshiva students from army service to the "Who is a Jew?" controversy, energetic religious vetoes have prevailed over the secular majority's predilections.

Grant Autonomy to the Various Camps in Clearly Defined Areas

Rather than imposing some obligatory national culture, consociationalism allows each group to live its own life in its own chosen way. Although issues of national identity are left vague and unresolved, the various communities enjoy substantial autonomy in areas such as education and internal organization. Intrusion into such autonomous zones is understood to constitute a casus belli, and the consociational style seeks to do what it can to avoid it.

A clear illustration can be found in the educational policy the Israeli leadership has pursued for many decades. Various forms of state-supported religious education—from national religious schools to Haredi—have been available to those parents who prefer it. Parallel to these religious educational systems, a secular or national education system serves roughly 75 percent of Israel's children.

Adopt Proportional Representation as a Voting System and as a Way of Allocating Resources

Proportional representation accurately reflects the distribution of opinion in society. Even relatively small "interest communities" stand a good chance of being represented. In systems of proportional representation, minority groups feel they are part of the political system and, therefore, tend to perceive the state as legitimate. Hence, proportional representation serves consociational purposes.

Majoritarian systems, by contrast, tend to undermine the ability of even large minorities to adequately express their needs and interests. Hence, adoption of a majoritarian system will be perceived by minorities as tantamount to disenfranchisement, that is, to denial of their electoral due.

In Israel, proportionality is perhaps the most deeply entrenched feature of its voting system. Despite the occasional failing attempt to introduce majoritarian voting, the proportional system, which has been with the Zionist enterprise since the first Zionist Congress more than a century ago, is broadly acknowledged as the most equitable way of expressing the multiple cleavages that divide Israeli society.

Form Broad-Based Coalitions That Include
Representatives of Opposition Camps

The classic rule of thumb declares that coalition-making parties prefer minimum winning coalitions. They provide the necessary means to rule without the need to dispense coalitional favors beyond what is absolutely necessary. Consociational democracy, by contrast, is marked by a tendency to create oversized coalitions, that is, coalitions larger than they need to be in purely arithmetic terms. To be sure, these extensive coalitions are not created to ensure short-term coalitional stability or even to immunize the coalitions from the demands of the smaller parties. Neither do these outsize coalitions express broad ideological partnership between its constitutive members. Consociationalism tends toward large, ideologically disparate coalitions because it aims at curbing potential conflict by drawing the opposition parties into the governmental ambit and, in so doing, strengthening the lines of communication between opposing factions. Large coalitions are consociationalism's way of channeling oppositional energies into nondestructive avenues and shoring up the legitimacy of the regime.

In the Israeli case, the consociational proclivity toward large coalitions with their conflict-allaying logic is especially prominent. For the first three decades of the state's existence, Mapai, the dominant party, regularly invited the National Religious Party to join its coalitions— even when it was patently superfluous arithmetically. Moreover, Mapai was prepared to go to great lengths—at times at substantial ideological cost to itself—to insure the participation of this dispensable coalition partner.

Favor Local and Administrative Solutions for
Contentious Issues of Principle

Issues raised publicly, at the national level, resist easy solution, for here the battle is joined not merely by contending parties with specific communal interests but at the symbolic and principled levels, as well. Each side's leadership digs in its heels, wishing to be seen as the stern guardian of communal values. Pragmatic politics, in which deals are brokered and concessions are made, disappears when the political process is exposed to public view. As a rule, symbolic public politics is the arena in which the militants of all sides thrive.

Transforming incendiary confrontations of principle into technical, functional, local, or administrative arrangements is, therefore, a primary strategy of consociationalism. Unlike public confrontations of principle that encourage do-or-die attitudes, the consociational style encourages the bureaucratization and localization of issues. At this more specific and concrete level, issues appear to be more tractable, compromises are easier to come by, and, generally, a more practical problem-solving (rather than a bombastic ideological) style prevails.

Israeli illustrations of this strategy are both prominent and frequent. For example, many of the most important religious services are dispensed at the local level, where the issues take on a more businesslike and less ideological tenor. (The attempts to bureaucratize religious contention is substantially addressed in much that follows.)

Transfer Politically Contentious Issues to Judicial Arbitration

Public issues requiring resolution are often too charged with symbolic and practical consequences to be handled effectively by the political system. Clear decisions on any side of an issue invariably ignite the wrath of the defeated group and encourage dangerous antisystem politics. When, however, these issues are transferred to the judicial system, they tend to take on a more neutral, legal, and technical character. Because the court system's deliberations possess an aura of formality and impartiality, because judicial decisions appear to be arrived at in accordance with some formal, nonpolitical code, they can, in certain important circumstances, be accepted by the losing party without setting into motion the familiar spiral of delegitimation.

Transforming political issues into judicial ones is an effective strategy only so long as the courts are judged to be a neutral, politically disinterested institution. However, when the courts produce what is perceived by certain groups to be a series of judicial decisions consistently hostile to their interests, the aura of bipartisanship fades, and the courts become political institutions like all others—with delegitimation a very real possibility.

In the past, judicial arbitration by Israel's Supreme Court was a favored means of resolving issues that were politically too hot to handle—so much so, indeed, that one authority warned against the "judicialization" *(mishpatizatzya)* of the Israeli political system.[17] More recently, however, the court has provoked the rancor of the Orthodox community with a series of decisions that were seen to favor a liberal Western rather than a specifically Jewish understanding of Israel's character. In Orthodox eyes, the courts have lost their standing as an unbiased mediator, with the predictable consequence: the erstwhile strategy of attempting to mitigate controversy by shifting political issues to judicial arbitration has in itself become charged and contentious.

Consociational Democracy: Favorable Conditions for Development

Consociational patterns are neither constitutionally entrenched nor legally mandatory: they are primarily behavioral and cultural. Most often, they develop over time as the result of felt need—partly by deliberate design and partly as the result of individual decisions that lack a general strategic conception.[18]

This is certainly true of the manner in which Israeli consociationalism evolved. Even when it is consciously instituted, consociationalism does not understand itself as the decisive resolution to communal strife. It does not intend to definitively pacify a polity's cleavages. At best, it seeks to systematize the manner of their expression and the way they are politically processed. By directing cleavage and conflict into manageable channels where mediation and compromise prevail, consociationalism blunts the sting of conflict without removing its source. In a word, despite consociationalism, deeply divided societies remain deeply divided. Conflict can, in very short order, burst aside the accommodationist patina and whirl out of control.

Clearly, not every deeply divided political community adopts a consociational style. Consociationalism has its fierce enemies as well as its dramatic failures. Militants on all sides can be expected to bridle against it and demand decisive victory. They will regularly deride the pragmatic, accommodationist "defeatism" of their more compromising comrades. Only when conditions are favorable does consociationalism succeed in frustrating the militant's designs. However, this begs the obvious question (with its obvious implications for the Israeli case): Which social conditions, historical contexts, and popular attitudes favor the success of consociationalism? The answers here are, to an extent, rather obvious, but they bear describing, nevertheless.[19]

At the level of political leadership, consociationalism requires, above all else, a deep loyalty to the very existence of the political system. Whether for historical, economic, or complex psychological reasons, the political system and its preservation must be a very high priority objective of the contending political elites. Where this commitment is lacking, there is little reason for leaders to moderate conflicts.

The leadership must also perceive and greatly fear the dangers immanent in unregulated conflict. Also necessary are the political will to overcome dissension and the prudence and initiative to develop appropriate mechanisms for its control. Finally, it is critical that the various elites have the requisite authority and resources to establish their control over potential opponents from within their own camp.

At the social level, a number of features supporting and reinforcing consociationalism have been identified. A threat from without galvanizes the sense of unity and encourages the accommodationist style. In this same spirit, a substantial nationalist movement that generates a sense of social solidarity between the community's constituent components also favors the development of accommodationist behavior patterns. When public attitudes are sensitive to and fearful of the fractured social system, the need for broad-based consociational coalitions enjoys a favored status.

It must be cautioned, however, that external threats act as consociational catalysts only when these threats are similarly perceived by all the polity's constituent subcommunities. Basic differences in assessing the danger from the external enemy or even serious disagreement as to how the danger should be dealt with may, in fact, render consociationalism more remote and unlikely. In such cases, certain parties to the internal conflict may actually exploit the fears of the external enemy felt by their political rivals in order to press on toward decisive victories.

Paradoxically, consociationalism is promoted when the cleavage lines dividing the political community into subcommunities are sharply defined rather than blurred. On its face, this appears to be perversely counterintuitive. It would seem that the more sharply defined are community lines, the more difficult consociationalist accommodation will be to establish. In the language of academic political science, it is "crosscutting" and not "overlapping" cleavages that encourage compromise. Regular contact, it is generally assumed, moderates conflict, just as greater social and ideological distance create more impervious barriers and a diminishing likelihood that complex social settlements will be hammered out.[20]

These intuitive conceptions are quite accurate but only in situations in which the various contending communities participate in the same political culture—when, whatever their differences, they agree about fundamental questions of identity and value. In such cases, contact does, in fact, promote compromise—rendering consociational arrangements superfluous. When, however, the ideological differences and social distance between the rival communities is so basic and principled that speaking of "the political community" in the singular is tinged with irony, consociationalism becomes a beckoning option. In such cases, it is precisely the social distance between the various groups that maintains stability and preserves some measure of civility between them; contact would create conflict at every turn.

Separation promotes stability by allowing each community to lead its own life, develop its own institutions, and create its own leadership without the friction-generating intervention of contentious rivals. In addition, without a leadership that is perceived as genuine and representative, the entire process of accommodationist negotiations and sanctioned intercommunal pacts will have great difficulty in getting off the ground. Having formed partially autarchic social systems and leaderships, the insulated community is now poised to negotiate social pacts with other similarly placed rivals. Leaders from each group, representing well-established communal interests and institutions, come to recognize that unregulated conflict would badly injure their own constituency's achievements. They appreciate the necessity for arrangements that insure their own autonomy by promising similar independence to their rivals. Communities that are socially isolated from one another recognize that for them to lead their own lives satisfactorily, they must, at least grudgingly, accept the same principle in regard to their antagonists. All of this takes place, of course, without their respective communities' growing any more fond of, or closer to, one another.

Consociationalism is, then, a manner of preserving the autonomy of ethnic, religious, linguistic, and regional groups by extending the principle of autonomy to other such groups and institutionalizing that autonomy in a complex social compact. Balanced against one another, potentially bellicose groups actually become concerned lest their rival's interests are seriously infringed. After all, the stability and welfare of the whole depends upon the minimal agreement and satisfaction of all parties to the accord.

In the ensuing chapters these preliminary descriptions of consociationalism are applied to religious-secular relations in Israel. What conditions promoted the rise of consociational arrangements during the Yishuv period and the first decades of statehood? What was the nature of the social compact agreed upon by the religious and secular communities, and how was it instituted? We contend that these enabling conditions and the consociational arrangements they produced have undergone significant transformations in the past two decades. Consociationalism as a regulative modus vivendi for religio-political conflicts has suffered serious setbacks, and its very existence is threatened. This decline in the politics of accommodation cannot as yet be described as a total rout or collapse, but there are clear signs that its staying power is being seriously undermined. The anxiety that lurks beneath the text of the chapters that follow centers on the apprehension that if consociationalism is indeed on its way out, the prospects for the Israeli future cloud over darkly.

Chapter Two

Consociational Democracy in the First Generation

This chapter surveys the consociational religio-political arrangements that prevailed during the first generation of Israeli public life. We take up such staples as the so-called status quo, the lack of a written constitution, army service, Sabbath laws, religious education, and the "Who is a Jew?" issue. For our specific methodological purposes, we understand the first generation as spanning the roughly thirty-year period from the establishment of the state in 1948 to the electoral upset that brought the Likud to power in 1977.

Coalitions and Consociationalism

One of the more doubtful platitudes of Israeli politics declares that the achievements of the religious parties have consistently derived from their ability to tip the coalitional scales in one direction or another. Without their participation, so it is said, either coalitions could not be formed or they would be so narrow as to be unworkable.[1] This hypothesis may well be accurate for the "two-camp" era beginning in the late 1970s and early 1980s, but it has little validity for the earlier "dominant-party" era.

During the earlier period of dominance by Mapai (Israeli Workers' Party—from which the present Labor Party derives), the religious parties did not tip the scales—they did not even come close to doing so. Indeed, the standard definition of a *dominant party* (the category regularly used to describe Mapai) entails that it has sufficient electoral clout to form ruling coalitions without being dependent upon small parties, especially not on those with hostile ideological programs. In this earlier period, Mapai could form coalitions as it saw fit. Nonetheless, it chose to include the religious parties for consociational reasons rather than because they were arithmetically indispensable.

A careful analysis of the ruling coalitions during the period of Mapai dominance demonstrates that in the overwhelming majority of these coalitions, the National Religious Party (the NRP, earlier called the Mizrahi) was not critical for achieving a parliamentary majority.[2] From a coalitional perspective, such behavior is irrational; consociationally, it makes perfect sense. As one writer puts it, "The open invitation to the NRP to join every coalition should be understood as an attempt to neutralize what might have become a powerful source of cleavage."[3]

The Status Quo

Probably the most familiar of these conflict-neutralizing, consociational arrangements is known as *the status quo*. It was apparently first suggested by Zerah Wahrhaftig of the Ha'Poel Hamizrahi Party shortly before the declaration of statehood. Wahrhaftig then served as the head of the national committee, the institutional body charged with implementing the transition from the Yishuv to the state. It had become eminently clear to the committee's members how fraught and intractable were the issues related to the proper place of Judaism in the Jewish state. Realizing that consensus on these explosive issues was unattainable, they settled on a functional compromise: the present circumstances (the status quo) would be "frozen."[4] What had prevailed in the Yishuv would prevail in the state. Observance in public institutions of kashrut—Jewish dietary laws—and the Sabbath would continue to be the rule. The dominance of religious law with regard to marriage and divorce would carry on, as well. Similarly, the position of the Yishuv's religious institutions and the independence of religious education would be preserved.

Whatever Wahrhaftig's intentions, freezing such a dynamic, highly charged, and many-sided reality was more in the nature of a declaration of principles than a specific or enforceable rule. The very transition from Yishuv to statehood posed a myriad of novel problems that could not be reduced to previously solved ones. Moreover, with zealous protagonists confronting one another, an aggressive, adversarial relationship was inevitable. It quickly became clear that a protean reality producing new dilemmas regularly could not be bound by so undynamic a principle as the status quo. Indeed, exactly what constituted the status quo became, in itself, a highly contentious issue.[5]

Nevertheless, the status quo does set down certain flexible guidelines that act as starting points for negotiation. They present a kind of default position with presumptive validity. Deviation is clearly possible, but it requires cogent justifications. Attempts to implement egregious departures from accepted practice begin, therefore, from a position of substantial disadvantage. The status quo having become entrenched in the public wisdom as the operative principle defining the position of religion in public life, changes in Israel's religio-political reality are, for the most part, incremental and cumulative.

Each subsequent change creates a new status quo that serves as the current starting point for further negotiations. In some issues, such as service of yeshiva students in the army, the Orthodox community has succeeded in pushing the line of the status quo in directions favorable to its interests. In other areas, such as Sabbath observance, the nonreligious communities have enjoyed the upper hand. What is important for our purposes is that there has scarcely been a deal cut, a compromise broached, or a coalitional agreement signed in religio-political matters that did not appeal to the status quo as the relevant regulative principle.

The status quo agreement represents Israeli consociationalism in its most visible, familiar, and enduring form. In addition, its persistence over the decades testifies clearly to its not being merely a stop-gap measure necessary during the tumultuous early years of statehood—a temporary cease-fire tactic in particularly trying circumstances. It has survived through five decades of intense religio-political strife and through tumultuous economic, political, and cultural changes.[6]

(It might be argued that had David Ben-Gurion not opted for a politics of conciliation but rather had pressed his advantage early on and insisted on a far sharper divide between religion and state, it might have substantially obviated many of the problems we face today. These kinds of "what if?" questions are, however, more entertaining than they are constructive. It cannot be denied that a decisive policy might have led to a resigned acceptance on the part of the religious leadership. Then again, it might just as well have precipitated an explosion with which the fledgling state was in no position to deal. In any event, questions such as this are not part of our concerns.)

Over the years, the status quo agreement has been consistently shot through with consociational elements. First of all, it avoids principled, decisive outcomes and encourages functional, "muddling through" agreements. Second, the non-Orthodox community, with its many powerful political parties, desists from exercising its clear majoritarian prerogatives. It refrains from forcing its will on the religious community. Third, all parties to the agreement recognize the existence of "red lines"—policies so inimical to communitarian interests (most often the religious) that adopting them would constitute an intolerable and system-threatening affront. Each community, in other words, retains the right of veto in regard to its own most pressing interests and sensitivities.

Desisting from Drafting a Constitution

In the Western liberal tradition, constitutions serve to limit the power of government and to protect individuals and minorities from the tyranny of the majority—especially from the depredations of agitated, populist majorities set on riding roughshod over minority rights.[7] Interestingly, Arend Lijphart sees constitutionalism of this kind as typical of consociational arrangements: it prevents dominant communities or even coalitions of communities from exercising their majoritarian prerogatives. For example, the Belgian and Swiss constitutions grant certain inviolate forms of cultural autonomy to its constitutive communities.[8] It would then seem, prima facie, that Israel's lack of a constitution is an anti-consociational feature that might well encourage majority-rule politics. However, this is not so.

Were the conflict in Israeli public life focused on the distribution of resources between the various communities—secular and religious—a constitution might, indeed, prevent the abuse of majority power. Such a conflict, however, would be quite mild in comparison with the struggle that actually divides Israeli society. A mere sectorial conflict, one focused mainly on questions of allocation, would have little of the passion and urgency that animate religious issues in Israeli public life. Indeed, if the issue in contention were allocating resources to support the bona fide religious needs of those for whom a religious life is critical, even secular militants would not raise vigorous objections.

The intensity of Israel's secular-religious conflict reflects the opposing visions these communities pursue in regard to the very nature of the Jewish state. What is at stake is a politics of Jewish identity, a struggle over ultimate values rather than distributory justice, over the whole rather than the parts. Indeed, even when questions of allocation are at issue, the more principled clash over the nature of the Jewish state prevents their being considered in a dispassionate or businesslike way. Inevitably, they assume all the ardor and intractability of struggles over high principles and ultimate values; and in struggles such as this, constitutions are formidable obstacles to consociational "muddling through."

Constitutions serve as the basic charters of political communities: they define the collective's fundamental credo, its character, its common denominator of values and goals. As such, constitutions raise the most crucial issues in their most principled form. Both in its declamatory objectives and in its more specific fleshing out of the state's parameters, the drafting of a constitution forces the issues. It does not allow explosive questions to remain ambiguous and obscure.

Whatever the complex of reasons for the nonadoption of a constitution in Israel, religious issues were certainly among them.[9] The Knesset debate analyzing the difficulties involved in drafting a constitution began with the secularist charge that "the religious bloc's fear of a constitution is the heart of the matter." Zerah Wahrhaftig retorted that the religious parties did indeed have serious reservations about a constitution. A constitution, he said, is "like a calling card that shows who this people is and what this state is"; and the constitution proposed by the secular side is "incapable" of expressing this unique character of the Jewish people. "We are known in the world," Wahrhaftig argued, "as the people of the Book of Books." A secular constitution will not "strengthen this tie to our rich past, but rather sever it." The leader of the Haredi group Agudat Israel, Rabbi Yitzchak Meyer Levin, was even more forthright: "The goal of religious Jewry is that only the laws of the Torah will be established in all areas of life in the state."[10] The implication was obvious: a written constitution would be either redundant or inadmissible— redundant if it established the laws of the Torah as the law of the land, inadmissible if it did not.

In the end, the drafting of a constitution was temporarily suspended— and the suspension has continued for half a century. Consociational considerations triumphed. Having been made public and principled through public debate, the complex of issues relating to a constitution was recognized as irresolvable. The religious community's opposition to a constitution was perceived as a "red line" that could not be crossed without system-threatening consequences. Despite its substantial majority, the non-Orthodox desisted from drafting a Western-style liberal constitution, that is, from a decisive resolution to the issue.

It was also clearly understood that a sharply articulated public charter would severely limit the room for maneuvering, compromising, and negotiating that would be available to the contending parties. Leaving the most principled issues in a state of equivocal abeyance maximized the possibilities of creative consociational adaptation. How critical this principled ambiguity was became clear in the 1990s with the inception of what is today called the constitutional revolution.

The Yarmelke and the Beret: The Religious Camp and Army Service

Today, somewhere near 7 percent of each year's draft-age young men are not inducted into the Israeli army. Yeshiva students in Haredi institutions who declare that Torah study is their vocation are granted a deferment from service, which normally becomes a complete release after a few years. At the end of 1997, twenty-eight thousand such students were granted a deferment from service. The total number of yeshiva students deferred from service in the fifty years of Israeli statehood stands at just under seventy thousand.

From the Haredi perspective, the yeshiva's unique character, its indispensability to Jewish flourishing, justifies this controversial release from a near-universal obligation. A yeshiva, they explain, is not merely a school or a rabbinic seminary—not even a seminary with full-time dormitory arrangements. Yeshivas are total support systems and total socialization frameworks that aim at enclosing the student fully in the world of Halacha, learning, and holiness. The concepts of free time and vacations are entirely foreign to its purposes. Its avowed objective is to mold the student's character by totally controlling his environment. As Wahrhaftig has put it, the important thing about a yeshiva student is not what he *knows* but what he *is*.[11]

Hence, disrupting the course of study or adulterating the totality of the yeshiva environment by years of army service is seen as profoundly damaging to the yeshiva's entire raison d'être. The fact that prospective yeshiva students usually spend their childhoods within an insulated, often hermetically sealed world only adds to the dangers involved in army service. Were they drafted, the Haredi leadership declares, they would necessarily confront a secular majority and all manner of corrupting influences—not least of which would be exposure to women soldiers.

Historically, the origins of the deferments given to yeshiva students date back to the period of transition between the Yishuv and statehood.[12] Army leaders, although willing to accept compromise solutions in regard to army service of yeshiva students, were deeply reluctant to accede to the principle that a certain sector of the population would be exempt from defending the country. For their part, the major Haredi yeshiva deans (the *roshei yeshiva*) expressed sweeping and unconditional opposition to military service for their students. Leaders of the Haredi community argued that yeshiva students, by studying Torah, were contributing their fair share to the perpetuity of the Jewish people—a contribution equal to that of soldiers: in the wake of the Holocaust's destruction of the flower of the European yeshiva world, this small remnant ought to be encouraged in its attempt to reconstruct the world of Jewish learning.

The yeshiva leadership was, moreover, alarmed by the tendency to "erosion" in the young Haredi generation, their desertion of the yeshivot for greener pastures elsewhere. The very preservation of the Haredi community, they sensed, depended on their ability to insulate their young from the seductions of the modern world by completely controlling the critical period of their socialization.[13] (More cynical observers contend that their unwillingness to serve in the army reflects their basic hostility to Zionism and to Israel.)[14]

In a manner that is typical of consociational arrangements, the deferment of yeshiva students was never explicitly legislated. Despite the divisiveness of the issue, or perhaps precisely because of it, a clear legal locus for its authority is difficult to locate. In the end, the deferment of yeshiva students was appended to a technical provision in the Security Service Law, which stipulates that the minister of defense has the prerogative of postponing the date of a soldier's induction. Formally, therefore, the induction of yeshiva students is merely deferred; in practice, as noted earlier, deferment is usually tantamount to an eventual full release from army service.[15] Initially, only a few hundred students were involved. Over the years, and in no relation to their demographic growth, the numbers of nonserving Haredi men has soared to the point where it is no longer a peripheral matter either quantitatively or politically.[16]

Ben-Gurion's willingness to accept this controversial arrangement has been attributed to many sources. Initially, only about four hundred students were involved, and he, like many other secularists, believed (with remarkable credulousness as it turned out) that ultra-Orthodoxy would not survive in a modern and progressive Jewish state. Furthermore, he surmised that it would be only a short deferment; in the end, yeshiva students, too, would be inducted. It is also said that his unwillingness to clash with the Haredim was related, inter alia, to their being located largely in the city of Jerusalem, which was the highly sensitive focal point of a great many other fraught issues (related, for example, to the right-wing undergrounds of Etzel and Lehi) in the early state era.[17] Finally, he was moved by the desire to reconcile the various sectors of the Jewish people (especially the very hard-hit Haredi community) in the wake of the Holocaust.

This account of Ben-Gurion's assent to Haredi demands, it should be observed, focuses on causes related to the specific conditions prevailing in the early statehood period. Why, then, has exemption of yeshiva students endured for five decades despite the vast changes that have taken place? More pointedly formulated, how has it happened that a substantial portion of the population continues to be exempted from military service in a country where such service is considered to be one of the most (if not the most) important of a citizen's duties?[18] The question is even more trenchant because the secular majority could have rested its case comfortably on the national religious community that not only serves in the army but also deems nonservice to be crass draft evasion—indeed, condemns it as sinful.[19] (This argument becomes stronger still in the era of the *hesder* yeshivot, which combine yeshiva study with military service—but more on this later.)

Finally, the reasons that moved Ben-Gurion to accept Haredi military exemptions long ago ceased to be relevant. There have been, by now, tens of thousands of exemptions granted; it is no longer a paltry exception to the rule. Deferment has proved to mean exemption in practice. Jerusalem as the capital of Israel is an established fact. Last, the yeshiva world is no longer the "remnant" it once was: it boasts of more students today than in any other previous period in Jewish history. Neither can it be argued that the exemption has continued for coalitional reasons: Agudat Israel left the coalition in 1952 and, even when part of it, was never arithmetically critical to its viability.

Despite the disappearance of the initial motives, army exemptions have persisted, even expanded, without serious attempts to terminate the arrangement. Only consociational explanations are adequate to account for this singular phenomenon. The fear that system-threatening conflict would result from halting the arrangement rendered majoritarian politics immaterial, indeed, perilous. It was and continues to be understood that deference to the idiosyncratic needs of a small cultural community is difficult to avoid—however repugnant the arrangement may be to majority sensibilities.

For its part, the Haredi community makes it quite clear that nonservice is indispensable for its communal existence, a "red line" that may not be crossed. Without the independence and separatism granted by educational autonomy and exemption from service in the army, the viability of their communal existence—so they aver—is threatened in an intolerable way. Thus, despite the absence of coalitional motives, despite the centrality of army service in the Israeli ethos, despite the obsolescence of the initial motives, despite the fact that other religious communities do serve, army exemptions continue to be granted to Haredi young men. In fully consociational style, this critical arrangement is nowhere enshrined in law; it exerts its dramatic political influence from the obscurity of a technical administrative statute.

The national religious community, by contrast, feels that army service is an obligation—even a religious obligation. Nevertheless, the study of Torah remains their highest priority. To synthesize the two duties, the *hesder* (arrangement) yeshiva, which combines Torah study with army service, was created.[20] From its inception, the hesder yeshiva has become the most important form of service for graduates of the yeshiva high schools. It has become one of the flagship accomplishments of the national religious community and among the sturdiest of Israel's consociational arrangements.

National Service for Women: Haredim versus the National Religious

The issue of national service for women brought to the fore a significant cleavage within the Orthodox community. The Security Service Law provides for the obligatory drafting of women into the army while explicitly exempting religious women. The representatives of the Haredi Agudat Israel, Rabbis Yitzchak Meyer Levin and Kalman Kahana, expressed principled opposition to the drafting of all women without regard to their religious identification. In their view, the conscription of women

was not introduced because of military necessity; it was another strata-
gem utilized by secular modernists to create gender equality in an antireligious, "progressive" society.[21] In the end, lacking much choice in the
matter, Levin and Kahana reluctantly accepted the provision that expressly exempts only religious women.

In their opposition to the drafting of women for military service, the
ultra-Orthodox were joined by the national religious community. The
latter were not entirely comfortable with the position they adopted, however. They were discomfited by the feeling that in exempting religious
women from service they were being derelict in their duties as committed Zionists who supported the national efforts of the young state.
Hence, they urged their woman followers not to exercise their right of
exemption. They encouraged religious women to enter army service in
the framework of certain religiously sponsored military and agricultural
units *(nahal).*[22]

The conflict erupted in 1951, when Ben-Gurion proposed a revision
to the Security Service Law that would have compelled religious women
to prove their religiosity in order to exercise their exemption. More important still, he argued in favor of National Service units within the context of the Israeli Defence Forces (IDF), into which religious women
would need to be drafted. The Haredi camp rejected the proposal root
and branch. Within the national religious community, on the other hand,
it ignited intense controversy. The Chief Rabbis publicized an open letter
in which they prohibited the drafting of religious women into the army—
even in the context of National Service units. On the other side, important factions within the Ha'Poel Hamizrahi Party (comprising the religious kibbutz and La'mifneh) declared their support for national service
and censured the rabbis for their unwarranted conservatism. Typically,
these controversial proposals were never brought to the Knesset floor.

Months later a differently formulated proposal for national service
was raised by the minister of labor and welfare. It dissociated National
Service from the IDF and advanced the idea of implementing it within a
fully civilian context. The idea of national service in a nonmilitary context neutralized the objections of the Chief Rabbinate and strengthened
the position of the more liberal elements within the Ha'Poel Hamizrahi.
For its part, the leadership of the Agudat Israel persisted in its unconditional opposition: it withdrew from the coalition and set into motion a
series of strident demonstrations both in Israel and abroad. Although
the law, with the support of the national religious community, did finally

pass, it was never implemented, because it lacked the necessary executive regulations to be put into effect—regulations that were never prescribed.[23]

Consociational principles are clearly visible at all phases of the debate. The attempt to impose a decision through legislative majorities provoked a public storm, incited demonstrations, prompted the Agudat Israel to leave the government, and resulted in the nonexecution of the approved legislation. In the end, the issue was resolved on the administrative-technical level, which prevented the further exacerbation of Haredi animosity. Notably, coalitional considerations were irrelevant because the coalition remained stable and effective after the departure of the Agudat. Characteristically for consociational politics, each of the parties to the struggle was allowed to adopt the solution it found suitable. The Haredi camp succeeded in avoiding inclusion of its women in the National Service. The national religious chose to implement the idea despite the absence of legal compulsion to do so. At present, national religious women, on a voluntary but widespread basis, serve in the National Service under government aegis.

Observance of the Sabbath and Holidays

Sabbath observance was already a heated issue during the period of the British Mandate, and a number of compromise arrangements were adopted—arrangements that later served as the basis for the status quo agreement. It was decided that the Sabbath would be observed in the activities conducted by all national institutions. Public transportation would be suspended for the Sabbath in all cities except Haifa and Eilat (whose religious populations were small). Similarly, statutes prohibiting commerce and labor on the Sabbath were put into effect.[24] In the first official judicial document, adopted shortly after the establishment of the state (P'kudat Sidrei Ha'shilton ve'hamishpat 1948), it was declared that the Sabbath and Jewish holidays were the permanent rest days of the State of Israel. In 1951, the Working Hours and Rest Law was passed, and it was the focus of acute controversy.

For the Orthodox, halachic Sabbath observance is of cardinal significance. Both theologically and in terms of life rhythms, Sabbath observance is likely to be the litmus test for commitment to Judaism. By contrast, for the secular parties, compliance with the prohibitions and rites that Halacha enjoins for the Sabbath are alien and intrusive, not to say anachronistic. Although the latter support days of rest and periodic hol-idays, their justifications are more likely to be socialist or functional than halachic. To be sure, days of rest naturally coincide with those pre-scribed by the Jewish calendar, but their spirit was defined among secu-lar Jews by leisure and relaxation rather than by rigorous religious per-formance.

Inevitably, the differences eventuated in conflicting visions of what the Sabbath would look like in a Jewish state. For the Orthodox, it meant closing down all workday activities, from businesses to public trans-portation to places of public entertainment (cafés, restaurants, movie houses, theaters, sporting events, et cetera). They demanded the passage of a sweeping national Sabbath law that would prescribe Sabbath obser-vance in the spirit of Halacha. For the nonreligious, by contrast, public transportation and especially the availability of recreational facilities were the essence of a day of rest.

The controversy also related to business closure on the Sabbath. The Working Hours and Rest Law included the following provision: the minister of labor was authorized to permit work on rest days "if he is convinced that ceasing work . . . is liable to inflict major damage on the economy, on an ongoing work project, or on the provision of vital ser-vices to the public or to a part of it." Such exemptions would not be given to entire sectors of the economy without the express permission of a committee composed of the prime minister, the minister of religion, and the minister of labor.[25] Interestingly, the national religious commu-nity was internally divided on whether to support the law (the political leadership favored the bill, whereas Chief Rabbi Herzog opposed it). In the end, it passed; and for the ensuing decades, it has constituted the central legislative locus of Sabbath observance in Israel.

In practice, complex consociational arrangements regarding Sabbath observance have evolved—arrangements that have aimed at blunting, sidestepping, and defusing the explosive issues involved. Not surpris-ingly, controversy between the religious and the secular continued after the passage of the Working Hours and Rest Law: the secular attempted to give a liberal reading to the exemptions permitted, and the religious endeavored to restrict them. Over the years, the line of scrimmage has shifted in one direction and then in the other. In recent years, however, the balance has moved in the secularists' favor—indeed, many businesses and shopping centers simply ignore the laws and open on the Sabbath—

but it is still far from being a decisive victory. Indeed, as these words are being written, the minister of labor (Eli Ishay, from the Sephardic ultra-Orthodox party, Shas) is attempting, once again, to enforce the law.

The operation of recreational facilities and public transportation on the Sabbath have also been shunted into consociational channels. Notably, the functioning of recreational facilities on the Sabbath was never definitively dealt with in primary national legislation. The frontal collision between the positions of the religious and secular communities precluded such a resolution of the issue. Instead, the subject was transferred to the local level and to auxiliary municipal regulations. The substance of these regulations differed from place to place in accordance with the character of the local population and the power relations between the various local political associations.

In regard to public transportation, the status quo has continued to hold sway. Here too, interestingly, the arrangements that prevail are based not on written law but rather on informal agreement. True to consociational "muddling through," no secular criterion or halachic principle regulates the field. For example, bus transportation is largely prohibited, although taxi service is permitted. In homogeneously religious neighborhoods, no motorized transportation whatever is allowed. Typically, many other issues have remained mired in deliberate ambiguity. This lack of resolution has invited regular attempts from both sides to try the law's limits and to redraw the line at points more favorable to their own objectives.

A few illustrations will suffice. In the absence of public transportation on the Sabbath, attempts were made to provide transportation by truck from Jerusalem to Tel Aviv. In the course of a demonstration against this Sabbath transport, one demonstrator—apparently suffering from heart disease—died after being struck by a policeman's club. The public storm that ensued effectively ended the attempt to evade the law.[26] In 1962, the League against Religious Coercion petitioned the courts against the closure of certain Jerusalem streets on the Sabbath; its appeal was rejected by the Israeli Supreme Court. In 1970 an attempt was made to hold motorcycle and car races in Ashkelon on the Sabbath. A highly interesting resolution to the subsequent controversy was devised. The National Religious Party and Agudat Israel took it upon themselves to provide full financial restitution to the event's organizers in return for its cancellation. It was even suggested that a national campaign to raise the necessary funds would be undertaken. In the event, however, part of the religious leadership objected; they claimed that it was undignified to re-deem the Sabbath by payoffs.

Zerah Wahrhaftig affirms that the option of legislating a full-scale Sabbath law existed at a number of different junctures in Israeli politi-cal history. It would have strengthened the position of the religious com-munity, he contends, in its constant struggle against erosions in the sta-tus quo. Yet, paradoxically, the religious leadership of the Mizrahi Party had serious reservations about supporting an authoritative Sabbath law (and, in fact, such a law was never passed). The specific declaration, in a definitive document, that violations of the Sabbath (for example, trans-portation in Haifa and Eilat) were permitted in the Jewish state was deeply hateful to them. They preferred, in the spirit of consociational muddling through, to allow the push and pull of a complex demographic, cultural, and political reality to determine the outcome rather than to conclusively accept the idea of a "stunted Sabbath," that is, to condone retreat in matters of high principle.[27]

The Varieties of Religious Education

Secular-religious conflict ineluctably includes conflict over education. What counts as genuine education (and what as superstition or heresy) goes to the very heart of the matter. Not surprisingly, the religious Zion-ist Mizrahi Party was formed in 1901 in reaction to the Zionist move-ment's declaration that education was to be one of its most important functions. Secular Zionist education, the religious declared in protest, affronts our sensibilities both as Jews and as Zionists. When the Tenth Zionist Congress decided some nine years later that the movement's exec-utive committee would henceforth be in charge of organizing its educa-tional activities, certain Mizrahi members voiced the shrill demand that the party leave the Zionist movement in protest. Outvoted by the major-ity, the disaffected minority bolted the Mizrahi Party and contributed to the foundation of the Haredi, non-Zionist, Agudat Israel.

During the Yishuv era, the division of educational activities into three separate streams became the familiar compromise: a workers' stream under the aegis of the socialist camp, a general stream consisting of Zion-ists who were neither religious nor socialist, and the Mizrahi-sponsored national religious stream, which was both religious and Zionist (and oc-casionally socialist, as well). Alongside the various Zionist educational streams, the Haredi community operated its own educational institutions. This multicultural arrangement embodied the familiar consociational principle of communal autonomy: each sector directed its own schools according to its own beliefs without the intervention of the others. In 1949 this informal arrangement received legal confirmation in the Compulsory Education Law.

Despite its newly established legal status, however, the waves of immigration from the Middle East and northern Africa that inundated the fledgling state—doubling its population in the course of a few short years—confronted the "stream" arrangement with an entirely transformed sociological reality. The altered situation consisted in the unprecedented fact that the new immigrants *(olim)* were, for the most part, traditional and observant Jews. It was immediately understood by the veteran elites that the new olim, with their overwhelming numbers, had it in their power to shift the national balance in entirely new directions, away from the dominance of the secular-socialist camp. No wonder, then, that the various elites embarked upon a no-holds-barred campaign to control the socialization process of these potential constituents—especially the education of the younger generation. Each camp used whatever leverage it could muster to induce the younger olim to enter its own educational stream. It was not unusual for them to resort to means best described as blackmail. They often exploited the newcomers' lack of orientation in their new democratic surroundings, their innocence in regard to the difference between the parties and their ideological programs, and their dependence on the existing networks for work, housing, and the like.[28]

The struggle over the "soul of the olim" raged from 1949 to 1952. Although free individual and family choice among the available educational streams was the declared regulative principle, political activists and educators of the labor camp were alarmed at the prospect that they would lose their hegemony were the olim to gravitate (as well they might, given their traditionalism) toward religious educational institutions. Consequently, they attempted to prevent the establishment of religious schools in areas populated heavily by olim. In areas where religious schools already existed, they exerted various forms of pressure and offered all manner of inducements to impel the olim to register their children in the workers' educational stream. The religious parties reacted furiously. David Pinkas, a member of the Knesset for the Mizrahi Party, described what was taking place as "mental coercion and an inquisition against the faith of Israel . . . religious and cultural murder." He concluded that if these practices did not stop, "they would inevitably cause bloody civil war."[29] Against this charged background, the government set up the Commission of Inquiry Regarding Education in the Olim Camps, which submitted its report in May 1951. Its account of what had been taking place largely corroborated Mizrahi allegations of coercive tactics and the abuse of power.[30] Nevertheless, despite attempts to resolve the impasse, the struggle continued; indeed, it was the source of serious coalitional instabilities. In 1950, it had precipitated the government's resignation, and although the government was soon reconstituted, the rancor and turmoil left their tell-tale marks on the sensibilities governing the emergent political system. The crisis revealed the alarmingly destructive potential of such basic cultural conflicts—especially when ignited by demographic and social transformations that rendered older consociational arrangements no longer viable.

The Second Knesset struggled with passing a national education law meant to set the educational domain on a new and more stable footing. After intense negotiations, a bill characterized by complex compromises and concessions was finally accepted. Moreover, in an effort to assuage the stormy conflicts that had set religious against secular, a government made up of Mapai and the religious parties was formed. In consociational terms, it might be said that this coalition was dictated precisely by the intensity of the conflict that had preceded it. Moreover, in the negotiations, Mapai—despite its majority and its ability to form a coalition without the religious parties—yielded to their religious partners on a broad front of issues. The National Education Law provided for the abolition of the workers' stream and the general stream but for the preservation of the national religious stream. Mapai transferred its erstwhile control over the religious workers (a substream of workers' education) to the national religious parties.[31] There were, to be sure, declamatory pronouncements that henceforth the educational system would be fully "national" (mamlachti); in practice, however, autonomous religious education was the reality on the ground.

Of great interest is the law's formal recognition of the Independent Educational System (Chinuch Atzma'i), which was a direct continuation of the Agudat Israel school system.[32] This is one of the most enlightening of consociational agreements: the Haredi Independent Educational System would now be entitled to governmental budgetary largesse despite the fact that its curriculum was non-Zionist—and often anti-Zionist and expressly hostile to the State of Israel; that Agudat Israel was not a part of the coalition nor was its inclusion essential to coalitional majorities; and that Mapai already had religious allies who were themselves none too happy with Haredi education.

The "Who Is a Jew?" Issue

In terms of sheer notoriety, the "Who is a Jew?" controversy is probably the most salient and familiar of secular-religious issues in Israel. The passion it aroused (and, in different forms, still arouses) relates to the fact that it calls into question the very criteria of belonging to the Jewish people. For our purposes, it also incorporates consociational bargaining and compromise in a most illustrative way.

The legal background to the controversy begins in the very early years of statehood. The Law of Return (1950) proclaimed that "every Jew has the right to immigrate to Israel." According to the Statute for Resident Registration (Pekudat Mirsham Ha'toshavim), the details of an individual's religious and national identity are to be entered in the Population Registry, as well as on one's identity card.

From the religious-halachic perspective, there is no distinction between religious and national identity. One's Jewish identity, in this view, is measured not by the degree of one's faith or observance but rather by one's ethnocommunal origins: anyone born of a Jewish mother is Jewish, even in a total absence of faith (indeed, a total rejection of one's Jewish background), whereas a deeply devout individual lacking maternal Jewish origins is not. In sharp contrast, the modern secular view understands identity as a freely chosen, consciousness-determined quality that cannot be imposed by formal, external criteria such as those provided by Halacha. One is, in this view, what one says one is.

Given the threatening divergence in regard to so basic a subject as what constitutes national belonging, it is not surprising that even before the issue erupted into national attention, the various laws and statutes refrained from giving *Jew* a clearly determinate meaning. This deliberate ambiguity, however, invited incompatible interpretations and, finally, the intervention of an impatient government minister. In 1958, the minister of the interior (Yisrael Ben Yehuda, of the Achdut Avodah Party) formulated guidelines for the use of registry officials according to which any person who sincerely and honestly declared himself or herself a Jew would be registered as a Jew with no further evidence required.

Similarly, the testimony of parents who declare that their children are Jewish will be accepted—regardless of whether, by halachic standards, the parents are Jewish or not.

The National Religious Party insisted on the abolition of the guidelines and, when its demand was spurned, resigned from the government coalition in July 1958. Notably, the NRP's decision to leave the coalition had little or no coalitional significance; with the inclusion of the NRP, the government had a solid majority—80 members out of a 120-member parliament—and after its departure the coalition still numbered a comfortable 69. For nearly a year and a half the NRP remained outside the government. From every narrowly coalitional point of view, Mapai had no reason to court NRP support. And yet it did.

In the wake of the outcry of the religious community, an unprecedented procedure was proposed by Ben-Gurion. The government would create a ministerial committee empowered to pose the question, "Who is a Jew?," to fifty leading Jewish scholars and religious leaders *(chachmei Yisrael)* worldwide. Moreover, the government pledged to abide by the majority decision. Of the forty-five responses received, thirty-seven supported the Orthodox definition.[33] (Some contended that the choice of respondents was rigged so as to yield an outcome congenial to the NRP.) The government thus retreated dramatically from the guidelines it had formerly accepted and in so doing demonstrated the depth of its consociational commitments.

The crisis ended with the December 1959 elections and the creation of a new government. Once again, Mapai did not require the coalitional services of the NRP to constitute a stable government. Indeed, in the interim, support for the existing coalition had risen from sixty-nine to seventy-four members. Yet Mapai and its partners expended considerable efforts to have the NRP join. Given the lack of coalitional grounds to account for these efforts, explanations must be sought in the drive to renew and revive the weakened consociational pact between the secular-socialist and the religious communities.

The question of registration guidelines was resolved in a typically consociational way, that is, without any decisive legislation or principled declarations. Moshe Shapira, leader of the NRP, was given the post of minister of the interior, and he simply canceled the guidelines forthwith. In their place he circulated new directives appropriate to the religious worldview of his party.[34] From then on, notably, the Ministry of the Interior has virtually always been controlled by the religious parties.

Shapira's new directives were tested almost immediately. Oswald Rufeisen (more commonly known as Brother Daniel), a Jewish survivor of the Holocaust who had converted to Catholicism and become a Carmelite monk, applied to come to Israel as an *oleh* (immigrant), to become a citizen, and to be registered as a Jew. He claimed that his national identity was Jewish despite his Christian religious affiliations. When the Ministry of the Interior refused Rufeisen's request, he appealed the decision to the Israeli Supreme Court. His petition was rejected by a four-to-one majority. Interestingly, the court's decision avoided religious arguments; it rested instead on sociological considerations. It contended that, on the one hand, the proper test for an individual's Jewishness in cases such as this ought not to be halachic. On the other, however, neither was it entirely a matter of personal choice. The intuitive perceptions of the Jewish community at large had to supply the relevant yardstick for communal membership; and from this perspective it was clear that Jews, both religious and nonreligious, do not consider a Catholic monk to be a Jew, whatever his personal feelings or biographical particulars. Although religious desiderata were not the decisive element in the court's decision, the religious community expressed satisfaction with the outcome of the litigation.

It was perhaps inevitable that this kind of secular-sociological criterion of Jewishness did not set the matter to rest, indeed, that it ended by begging the question all the more intensely. In 1968, Benjamin Shalit, an officer in the Israeli Army, applied to have his children—born of a non-Jewish mother—registered as Jews in the nationality category and as "without religion" in the religion category. Refused by the Ministry of the Interior, he appealed to the Supreme Court. The court, then in a mood of "judicial restraint," recoiled from dealing with an issue so close to the quick of national concerns. In the course of the proceedings, the reluctant court even suggested evading the issue by entirely omitting the category of nationality from the Population Registry—a proposal promptly declined by the government.

In early 1970 the court decided by a five-to-four majority that Shalit was in the right and that the Ministry of the Interior directives lacked a legal basis. The ministry was ordered to register Shalit's children as Jews nationally and, in the religious category, as without religion. Using the identical test they had used in the Brother Daniel case, they concluded

that Shalit's children, brought up as Israelis, speaking Hebrew, and cel-
ebrating Jewish holidays, were broadly perceived as Jews by the Jewish
population of Israel.

The outcome of the public tempest aroused by the Shalit case forced
the political system to deal with the question of Jewish identity in national legislation, a prospect from which consociational democracy
normally shrinks. Twenty years after passage of the Law of Return, the
Knesset defined a Jew as "one who was born to a Jewish mother or was
converted and is not a member of another religion."[35] Although clearly
a victory for the religious parties and a striking instance of consociational concessions to a cultural minority, there was a threatening (and
consociationally deliberate) ambiguity at the definition's center: what
was to count as a valid conversion? This, however, is to anticipate later
developments that are dealt with at length in subsequent chapters.

Consociational Democracy in a Dominant-Party System

Highlighting and demonstrating the uniqueness of secular-religious consociationalism is the striking absence of parallel arrangements anywhere
else in Israeli politics. Considering the tumultuous and imperiled conditions of Israel in its first decades of its existence—conditions that would,
ostensibly, encourage consensus-seeking and reciprocal concessions—
this absence makes clear that the religio-political arena represented a distinctive issue area in which special rules were understood to be mandatory. For example, consociational arrangements are not to be found in
the fierce ideological struggles between the dominant, Mapai-based coalition and its political opponents on the right and the left. Ben-Gurion
enunciated his nonconsociational policy in his famous guidelines for
coalition formation: "without Herut [the precursor of today's Likud] or
Maki [the Israeli Communist Party]." Neither do they have any reso-
nance in the national cleavage between Jews and Arabs—despite the fact
that the Arab community in Israel is, numerically at least, not very different in size from that of the religious. Here control, majority dominance, even repression and discrimination, are the prevailing paradigm.
Notably as well, consociationalism is foreign to the often troubled Ashkenazi-Sephardi cleavage.

Consociationalism stands out in its uniqueness when understood in
the context of Mapai dominance. Until 1977, Mapai triumphed, by a
wide margin, in every election campaign; it was the state-founding party,

with all the privileges accruing to that status, and it was in commanding control of the bulk of the state's power apparatus. Moreover, as a party at the ideological heart of Israel's political terrain, it could easily recruit adjoining parties for its coalitional requirements. Mapai was, therefore, not limited in its choice of coalition partners. This independence was demonstrated in its coalitional choices: once with the General Zionists to its right, and once with Mapam and Achdut Avodah that were to its left.[36] Notably as well, there was no single opposition party that represented a clear and threatening alternative to Mapai leadership—a fact that was widely recognized by the leading political actors at the time.[37]

All of which is to say that the consistent inclusion of the religious parties in Mapai coalitions cannot be accounted for by the standard rationales for power sharing. Mapai, as a dominant party, did not need the religious parties to further its ideological commitments or to realize its social programs. Its choice to, nevertheless, create a historical pact *(brit historit)* with the Mizrahi derives from premeditated cultural and consociational considerations. The manner in which these consociational ties begin to unravel during the two-camp era occupies our attention in the coming chapter.

Chapter Three

Old Issues, New Politics
The Second Generation

This chapter and those that follow examine the various factors that are weakening the consociational style in Israeli public life. Each factor, in and of itself, is insufficient to account for the major transformations that are intensifying the struggle over Jewishness in the Jewish state. Cumulatively, however, they achieve critical mass.

In this chapter we take up the political, electoral, ideological, and party-related factors that have contributed to the decline of consociationalism. These are: (1) the transition from a dominant-party system to a balanced two-bloc system; (2) the growing empowerment of the religious, especially the Haredi parties—their transformation from minority parties with limited prerogatives to parties with influence sufficient to determine the nature of the ruling coalition; (3) broad structural and ideological changes within the religious camp; (4) changes in the relative strength of the national religious and Haredi camps; (5) the growing tendency of the national religious community toward "Haredization" and political hawkishness; and, finally, (6) the transition from a political system characterized by crosscutting cleavages to one marked by overlapping cleavages in regard to the critical issues of collective identity, national boundaries, et cetera. All of these changes, we argue, undermine the requisite public disposition as well as the necessary objective conditions that support the successful implementation of consociational democracy.

From a Dominant-Party System to a Balanced Two-Bloc System

The political upset of 1977 in which the Likud rose to power represents a watershed in the dynamics of Israeli politics. For the first time since the earliest political stirrings in the Yishuv era, the dominance of the labor movement (Mapai, the Alignment, and the Labor Party) was successfully challenged. The balanced two-bloc political system that replaced dominance, and which continues to this day, exhibits a number of essential features.[1] First, there is a persistent electoral stalemate between the two large parties, Likud and Labor. Second, the system is marked by the presence of smaller "satellite" parties that are clearly identified with one of the large parties and have difficulty joining coalitionally with the other. In regard to the Likud, these satellite parties were Tehiya, Tzomet, Moledet, and the National Religious Party. The Labor Party's certain allies are Meretz and the various Arab parties. Third, the Haredi parties, and most especially Shas, although closer ideologically to the Likud, are able, at least in principle, to cooperate with either of the large parties. Fourth, when the electoral support of the various satellite parties is added to the constituencies of their preferred large parties, the two camps that are created are also remarkably balanced in support and, what is more, they have exhibited exceptional stability for more than two decades. Notably, even when the dead-heat balance between the two major parties is breached, such as in the election to the Thirteenth Knesset (1992), when Labor outpolled the Likud by twelve seats, the overall balance between the two blocs was nevertheless preserved.

The deep structural transformations occasioned by the rise of a balanced two-bloc system have had inevitable consequences for consociational politics. In the period of dominance, party competition was not especially intense: because there was little doubt about which party and camp would triumph, the competition, such as it was, focused on secondary issues, such as what the relative distribution of parliamentary representation would be, which parties would join Mapai in the coalition, and what payoffs they would receive.

A balanced two-bloc system, by contrast, is an intensely competitive system. With each side in striking distance of victory, zero-sum-game belligerence and contentiousness is much in evidence. Moreover, when elections are regularly won by razor-thin majorities (as in May 1996), the struggle over each vote can easily take on a do-or-die quality.[2]

Prima facie, it is tempting to hypothesize that conditions of party dominance will encourage decisiveness whereas balanced two-bloc competition will promote political dialogue and accommodation. After all, what more supports resolute action than clear majorities, the absence of viable alternatives, and the weakness of the opposition? On the other hand, accommodation would seem to be the eminently reasonable strategy in conditions of intense competition, when the need to recruit allies is of paramount importance. In more concrete terms, Mapai, with its non-religious and antireligious allies (Mapam, Achdut Avodah, the Progressives), could have passed whatever secular legislation it pleased. In the post-1977 balanced two-bloc system, by contrast, each of the large parties was intensely beholden to the religious parties, without whom they could not form a coalition. Neither of the large parties could adopt an electoral or coalitional strategy that left the religious communities out of its calculations.

But first impressions here are misleading. The central paradox of Israeli consociationalism consists in the fact that, on the ground, the logic cuts the other way. It is precisely the balanced two-camp reality—despite the need it creates for religious allies—that weakens the dynamics of consociationalism, just as party dominance, despite its apparent potential for decisiveness, creates the sustaining circumstances in which consociationalism can flourish.

The politics of accommodation that animates the consociational style, we have posited, is based on mutual adaptation, compromise, and deference. In essence, it rests on the controlling voice of the moderates and pragmatists in each camp. But how does a temperate voice dominate when deep cleavages create deep passions and deep passions tend to create a radical political style? The key to this paradox lies in the moderating influence of the dominant party—both on its own members and on the opposition's constituency.

Small parties, as radical as they may be, are fully aware of the dominant party's ability to form a variety of differently constituted coalitions. In such circumstances, militancy carries no clout; indeed, it is actually quite counterproductive. Radical demands on the part of small parties will, more likely than not, entail forfeiting coalitional participation—with all its attendant political rewards. Because the dominant party can avail itself of coalitional alternatives that exclude the contentious party, pragmatism turns out to be the most rational policy.

Mapam presents a clear illustration of this moderating dynamic. In the first generation, Mapam's stance on religion and state was radically secularist. Nevertheless, the party usually desisted from pressing its agenda on Mapai. Ultimatums in the spirit of its ideological principles were understood to be impolitic—carrying with them the danger of being exiled to the political wastelands. The distinction between "optimal objectives" and "what the traffic will allow" was regularly impressed upon the Mapam leadership. Mapai, for its part, demonstrated its willingness to form coalitions with only the religious parties, even to include the General Zionists, rather than accede to the troublesome demands of Mapam, its ostensible ideological neighbor. Hence, even when the electoral power of the avowedly secular parties was substantial, the existence of a dominant party prevented the conversion of this power into policy outputs, that is to say, into decisive political determinations. Moreover, against the background of dominance, the concessions that Mapai made to the religious parties were perceived as specific and restricted in scope—tactical compromises that did not challenge the basically modern and democratic nature of the state.

Much the same can be said of radical demands emanating from the religious camp. Religious values are understood to be absolute, and the tendency to present them in ultimative fashion is, therefore, only to be anticipated. Pragmatism has only a limited rationale in religious dialogue, particularly in the case of Orthodox Judaism. Besides, the party leadership needs to consider the positions of their religious authorities, who, it should be added, are free of the political constraints that control and circumscribe political leaders.[3] This tendency to political unconditionality is neatly illustrated by Agudat Israel's departure from the coalition in 1952—against the background of rebuffed religious demands.

After the declaration of statehood, within the national religious camp all manner of demands were raised, the combined upshot of which was converting Israel into a Torah state run according to halachic law. It is not difficult to imagine how discourse between the religious minority and secular majority would have been conducted had this vision of a Torah state been understood as the operative religious objective. It would have broken down as soon as it started. The readiness to compromise would have foundered, and the motivation for consociational arrangements would have entirely dried up. In practice, however, the moderate, pragmatic, political wing of the national religious camp triumphed over its radical rabbinical opponents, and the foundations of consociational democracy were set securely into place. Needless to say, appeal to the unavoidable political constraints involved in dealing with a dominant party were the most potent justificatory argument in the pragmatists' arsenal.[4]

The ability to neutralize the radicals declined dramatically with the rise of a balanced two-bloc system. Intense competition deriving from the finely balanced electoral stalemate renders each vote and each seat in the Knesset potentially critical. In such circumstances, no party can surrender any source of support—radical though it may be. Ben-Gurion could regularly iterate his coalitional maxim, "without Herut or Maki," and still have substantial maneuvering room for coalition formation. He could dismiss and disempower the radicals because he possessed adequate support without them.

This world is no more. The large parties now need to navigate their way through a very different network of constraints. They must desist from offending the extremists for fear that in so doing they will undermine their shaky electoral and coalitional prospects. After all, the radicals are, necessarily, an integral and critical part of their strategy of victory. On the right, for example, the Moledet Party was included into a Likud-led coalition, and its leader, Rehavam Ze'evi was even appointed minister. On the left, the influence of the Arab parties, upon whose (extracoalitional) support the Labor coalition relied during the 1992–96 government, rose to unprecedented heights.

It must also be emphasized that the direct election of the prime minister, which created, for the first time, a single national constituency, transfers the need to appease the radicals from the level of the party to that of the public at large. One clear illustration of this phenomenon took place in the weeks leading up to the May 1999 elections. Despite the fact that Aryeh Deri, the political leader of the Shas Party, had been convicted of major crimes and sentenced to four years in jail, the three leading candidates for the prime ministerial post were remarkably circuitous in regard to the question of whether they would negotiate with Deri if they won the election. The attorney general, Elyakim Rubenstein, referred to this unaccustomed quiet as "the silence of the lambs." Indeed, only when the public outcry became shrill did Ehud Barak and Yitzchak Mordechai expressly disqualify Deri as a negotiating partner.[5]

In sum, the balanced two-camp structure and the sharply competitive strategies it mandates encourage a decisive political style that subverts consociational accommodation. The mark (inter alia) of Israeli consociational politics is the prevalence of broad, conflict-defusing coalitions containing representatives of different and opposing camps. With the important exception of the so-called National Unity governments, coalitions in the balanced two-camp period tended to be based on relatively narrow majorities and on the ideological proximity of its constituent partners. Notably, these governments did not hesitate to take one-sided actions in regard to highly sensitive and critical matters. The Likud, for example, supported a major settlement campaign in Judea, Samaria, and Gaza. For its part, the Labor coalition initiated the Oslo peace process. In what follows we shall see that this trend toward decisiveness increasingly characterized the religious parties, as well—most especially, the Haredi parties, who rose to new levels of influence and power during this period.

The Changing Role of the Religious Parties in a Two-Camp System

During the period of Mapai dominance, the power of the religious parties, like that of other minority parties, was limited and conditional. Mapai acquiescence to religious needs related more to Mapai's socio-ideological calculations than to the decisive coalitional leverage exerted by the religious community. Moreover, concessions to the religious parties did not, in Mapai's eyes, constitute a threat to the fundamentally modern and democratic nature of the Jewish state.

From the religious parties' perspective, limited power dictated a political agenda of limited ambitions—which, in turn, deterred the nonreligious parties from feeling threatened by aggressive religious intentions. It was clear, furthermore, that in conditions of dominance, Mapai's willingness to meet religious needs derived from authentically consociational motives rather than from the ordinary calculations demanded by coalitional politics.

In the current balanced two-camp system, interparty dynamics are essentially different, both in structure and in content. First of all, as opposed to the National Religious Party, acting as the political representative for religious concerns as in the period of dominance, today the more aggressive and less mainstream Haredi parties are the dominant force. Second, whereas the NRP did not have decisive coalitional leverage, the Haredi parties do—they tip the scales in one political direction or the other. It has become axiomatic in post-1977 politics that to secure power and retain it over time, the cooperation of at least some religious and especially Haredi parties is of cardinal significance.

Notably, in the elections for the Thirteenth Knesset, Labor controlled a blocking opposition that precluded the possibility of a Likud-led coalition. Yet, with the sixty-one seats of Meretz and the Arab parties in its camp—the latter supporting Labor but from outside the government— the government of Yitzchak Rabin courted Shas and expended great energies in having it join the government and, after joining, in appeasing its demands. In all the previous processes of coalition formation in the 1980s, the situation had been starker still: without at least one of the religious parties—often more—it was impossible to achieve even a minimal majority in the Knesset.

Why has consociationalism been impaired by this new reality? Why does the more powerful current position of the religious parties negatively affect the politics of accommodation? To adequately answer this question we need to distinguish, at least analytically, between two different levels of inquiry: that related to the general atmosphere and prevailing political temper, on the one hand, and that of the practical political consequences, on the other. There can be little doubt that the balanced two-camp system creates a novel public attitude toward religious needs, religious agendas, and the religious parties. Religious demands, whatever their content, are currently perceived as resting upon the decisive coalitional leverage of the religious parties—especially the Haredi parties.[6] It matters little for our purposes whether this image accurately represents the reality: the perception of political "extortion" and "blackmail" has become so deeply rooted and prevalent that it possesses momentum of its own. Even were we to find, after painstaking empirical research, that the current position of the religious parties did not occasion an increase in the level of demand or lead to greater acquiescence on the part of the secular parties, the perception of the religious (Haredi) parties as illegitimately influential would continue nonetheless.

Let us imagine for the sake of illustration that one of the large parties decides to accede to the needs of the religious community out of genuinely consociational motives. Let us say, furthermore, that it proclaims its accommodating intentions explicitly and insistently. Will these motives and proclamations be accepted at face value, or (far more likely, of course) will they be interpreted as a verbal fig leaf with not-so-hidden coalitional objectives? For example, Ehud Barak (appointed leader of the Labor Party in 1997) based his electoral strategy upon (inter alia) a reconciliation with the religious community. Whatever his real intentions may be, however, his policy has been universally interpreted as a necessary political strategy dictated by coalitional realities. Even if there are authentic consociational motives at work here, they are obscured by skepticism born of political analysis. Thus, consociationalism, even if it does continue to sway the occasional political actor, is condemned to lead an occluded existence.

The fact that the religious parties have sufficient influence to tip the political scale in one direction or another does not, in itself, create this dominant public image. The source of the prevalent conviction that the religious parties are too powerful and "extortionist" in character derives from the political payoffs they regularly receive. To take a single example: Since 1977, it has become set practice for the Likud, whenever it forms a coalition, to delegate the Ministry of Education to the National Religious Party. It hardly needs adding that in conditions dominated by a bitter struggle over Jewish identity and cultural direction, control over the educational system is a strategically potent political asset.

Interestingly, in the first decades of Israel's existence, the National Religious Party was given control over national religious education. This is entirely congruent with the consociational idea of communal autonomy. The Haredi community, as well, was effectively in control of their own educational network, the Independent Educational System, as it is called. The secular parties posed no systematic objection to either of these institutionalized "autonomies."[7]

By contrast, from the time that Zevulun Hammer was appointed minister of education in 1977, secular fears of insidious religious influences in education have been regularly expressed. When Hammer, who served (until his passing at the beginning of 1998) as minister of education in Benjamin Netanyahu's government, tried to set up an Administration for Value-Centered Education, secular fears of a concerted effort at Judaizing the school system escalated. Struggles over his appointments to the new administration were waged between secular and religious forces in what was understood by the protagonists to be a zero-sum contest. Anxieties over religious intentions went so deep that calls for establishing a department for "secular humanist" education that would enjoy the same autonomy as religious education became the order of the day.[8] In a word, secular defensiveness was no longer exceptional; perceptually at least, the religious-secular contest was understood to be a winner-takes-all engagement.

In terms of "scale-tipping"—the power to effect political outcomes— the Haredi parties' position is considerably more salient and dramatic than that of the NRP. The latter effectively weakened its strategic position in coalition negotiations by moving ideologically in a hawkish and messianic direction. It has become a satellite party to the Likud, and, with few other available options, its bargaining leverage has suffered substantially. On the other side, Shas and Agudat Israel are effectively poised to fully exploit their parliamentary influence. They make no secret of the fact that they are, in principle, prepared to strike strategic alliances with either the Labor Party or the Likud.

Never was this willingness more apparent in principle and more appalling in practice than in what became known as the "stinking scheme" (targil masri'ach).[9] In 1990, Shimon Peres and the Labor leadership colluded with Shas to cause the fall of the Yitzchak Shamir government. Shas's parliamentary faction agreed to absent itself from a crucial confidence vote that would have denied Shamir his legislative majority. At the same time, Peres turned to Agudat Israel and invited it to join a new coalition under his leadership. But the elaborately concocted plans went badly awry. In the end, two members of the Agudat Israel refused to join a Labor coalition, thereby thwarting Peres's designs. This led directly to Shamir's forming a government that included, inter alia, both of Peres's erstwhile coconspirators, Agudat Israel and Shas. Their strategic availability to both potential coalition makers could not have been more dramatically demonstrated.

For some three months the political system was mired in the most vicious impasse in Israeli parliamentary history—a tragicomedy played out before an increasingly disgusted and demoralized population. They witnessed a politics of empty promises and cold-blooded betrayals, of renegades crossing party lines in return for political and financial favors, of cynical political deals that raised extortion and corruption to unprecedented levels—what can only be described as a shameless and grotesque farce. The part played by the religious parties in all of this was significant but hardly exclusive; it must be emphasized that the "war of all against all" style that prevailed in those tumultuous months left few political camps entirely untarnished. Nevertheless, the public imagination fastened especially on Haredi machinations. The sense that this "outsider" community, with values and lifestyles so different from those of the country's mainstream, was cynically cashing in on its coalitional indispensability became a bitter cliché. They were parlaying what was a serendipitous arithmetic fact into a degree of influence and control that was, in the eyes of many, simply obscene—a case, as the common phrase has it, of the tail wagging the dog. So deep was this sense of outrage that the Movement for Changing the Form of Government (a largely academic group with constitutional reforms as their objective) succeeded in organizing one of the largest demonstrations in Israel's history.

Another pointed illustration of the scale-tipping power of the religious parties can be found in the formation of the National Unity governments of the 1980s, especially the second such government, created after the 1988 elections. The results of the 1988 election made it clear that although the Likud could, arithmetically, form a government, to do so would involve intricate negotiations with a number of small right-wing parties and, especially, with four religious parties: the NRP, Agudat Israel, Degel Hatorah, and Shas. Haredi ultimatums in regard to the "Who is a Jew?" question proved to be so incendiary and crisis provoking that Shamir preferred to forgo the possibility of creating a narrow Likud-led coalition and chose instead to join Labor in a National Unity government. The public awareness of and unhappiness with Haredi power, the increasingly bold Haredi attempts to translate the strategic arithmetic position it commanded into unpopular coalitional payoffs, rose to new heights.

Yet all of this is mild by comparison with the explicit Haredi exploitation of their coalitional indispensability in the 1990s. If Haredi influence in the 1980s was a familiar but still episodic and often subdued presence, in the following decade it became a political weapon that was vociferously, even menacingly, brandished. In 1997, for example, the leader of the Labor Party, Ehud Barak, proclaimed that if and when he became prime minister he would act to have the Haredim and the Arabs conscripted in a National Service corps. The response of Shmuel Halpert of Agudat Israel was simple: "Let Barak not forget that the religious parties tip the scale in every coalition." Even more self-confident and conclusive was the rejoinder of Avraham Ravitz: "For so long as Barak's proposal is tabled, he will not be prime minister."[10] It may well be that the Haredi politicians read the political map accurately; they may, indeed, be quite as powerful as they believe. Yet their attainments and influence are clearly not the result of consociational deference. They command the power they do because of their coalitional indispensability and because of the winner-takes-all strategy they pursue.

All of this relates primarily to the way the religious-secular conflict is viewed by the public at large. From an erstwhile politics of accommodation, Israeli public life now is widely perceived to be dominated by a politics of decisiveness. It is true that many political leaders continue to act with the accommodation paradigm as their operative guide—for example, they will not abandon the status quo principle in their public discourse, often not even in practice—but for how long can such principles survive when public attitudes and popular cultural perceptions have undergone such a fundamental shift? There is all the difference in the world between a large and self-confident majority that is willing to defer to minority groups for the sake of public harmony and these same large groups that understand themselves to be coerced and effectively blackmailed by a minority that exploits its bargaining advantage to obtain policy payoffs that are odious to the majority of Israeli citizens. Consociationalism, even where it does survive as a motive and a strategy, is being progressively overwhelmed by the dynamics of the balanced two-camp system.

The Changing Roles of the Haredi and National Religious Camps

The rise of the Haredi parties to their current "scale-tipping" position took place against the background of far-reaching changes in the religious camp generally. To better assess the uniqueness of the present state of affairs, we need to present a short checklist of the most significant attributes of religious politics as it was practiced during the country's first generation. Electorally, there was great stability and continuity in the religious camp: the NRP represented the national religious camp, and the Agudat Israel and Po'alei Agudat Israel were the Haredi representatives. The NRP consistently received ten to twelve seats in the parliament, about two-thirds of the religious representation in the Knesset, and the Haredi parties received four to six, roughly a third. The Agudat Israel remained in opposition and enjoyed the fruits of consociational deference—for example, financial largesse to its educational system and the nonconscription of yeshiva students. The NRP was a virtually permanent coalition partner, and most of the consociational accommodations regarding religious issues were hammered out between the NRP and Mapai. The national religious community was essentially modern and open to the contemporary world, whereas the Haredi community was marked by high levels of cultural isolationism. The Haredim were also impassive toward government policies that did not directly affect their lives. Hardly a single one of these realities holds true as the century draws to a close.

The political upset of 1977 (in which the Likud replaced Labor as the coalition-forming party) foreshadowed the return of Agudat Israel to the coalition for the first time since 1952. Henceforth, the NRP would no longer be the single religious party in the coalition. Even more disastrous for the NRP was the dramatic loss of half its electoral power in the 1981 elections, down from ten to twelve seats in previous elections to a maximum of six (until 1996, when the number rose to nine). During the 1980s, moreover, the Shas Party's rise to prominence tellingly changed the composition and internal balance of religious representation in the Knesset: the NRP now controlled only a third of religious Knesset seats, the Haredi parties holding the remaining two-thirds. The peak of this process (at least until the present) was reached in May 1999 when the Haredi party, Shas, with seventeen seats, became the largest of the religious parties and the third-largest party in the Knesset, after the Likud and Labor.

These electoral transformations undermined the basis of consociationalism because the Haredi parties lack the very qualities that made accommodation with the first-generation NRP such a beckoning option. Consociationalism's viability rested upon the character of the parties that implemented it: the NRP and Mapai. Moderation and political pragmatism in foreign and social policy made the two parties natural allies. Religious differences were ironed out in the light of other important areas of consensus. Consociational arrangements followed almost as a matter of course. The rule of thumb dictated religious concessions in return for a relatively free hand in other issues, and this made for a long-term, mutually profitable compact. Religious concessions were relatively easy to make to a community with which the majority had myriad social, business, and neighborly ties, one that had been an active and integral part of the Zionist project, one that was, in many areas, similar in attitude and lifestyle to the majority. In more prosaic terms, it is far easier for ordinary secular Israelis to accommodate the needs of one with whom they have shared an army tent and gone on maneuvers in the reserves than to defer to one who does not serve in the army, disqualifies the Zionist project in principle, and with whose community they have no social contacts.

Hence, the reality that encouraged accommodation in the first generation has been badly battered. Not only has the national religious camp distanced itself from the political center with its settlements and its "greater land of Israel" campaigns, but the Haredi parties have become the main articulators of religious interests in the Knesset, as well. The first-generation NRP that strove for religious advantage but was not understood as a threat to the secular majority has given way to a radical religious protagonist whose objectives are perceived to be incompatible with those of secular Israel. Moreover, religious concerns are now advanced by a group who are popularly perceived as non-Zionists, who do not share the defense burden, and with whom the ordinary Israeli has little in common (and who, as we shall see below, are also perceived as parasitical freeloaders on other people's labor). In such circumstances, the willingness to defer and compromise is no longer what it was.

Secular public wisdom now has it that compromises are part of a slippery slope leading—if the Haredim get their way—to the eventual "Haredization" of the country. There is no point in compromise when each accommodation is perceived by the secular majority as part of "salami tactics"—cutting one slice at a time—the ultimate objective of which is quite clear. In such circumstances, digging in and taking a stand is deemed the more honorable and effective strategy. Yossi Sarid has expressed this new, anticonsociational attitude with a clarity and sharpness that recommend it as a summary of growing parts of the secular community. "One does not deal with the religious and Haredi establishment through flattery, doffing one's shoes respectfully, and namby-pamby sweet talk. You speak to them in the one language they understand—the language of resolute and relentless struggle."[11]

Beyond changes in styles of discourse and attitude, there have been important practical transformations that have contributed to a worsening of relations. One striking example involves the unprecedented appointment by Netanyahu in 1996 of Eli Ishay, of the Haredi Shas Party, as minister of labor and welfare.[12] This appointment accurately reflects the growing power of the Haredi community in Israeli politics as well as their increasing involvement in areas that they previously disdained as mundane, professional, and mainstream—that is, unsuited to Haredi interests and skills.

Practically as well, this appointment carries with it important consequences for religious-secular relations. The minister of labor is charged with enforcing laws related to hours of work and rest, more specifically, with enforcing those laws that prohibit work on the Sabbath and religious holidays. For the previous decade and more (even under a Haredi deputy minister of labor), laws forbidding the opening of businesses and places of entertainment such as theaters and cafés were enforced slackly, if at all. In many places in Israel—particularly those with a dominant secular character—these laws were entirely ignored. Shopping malls, restaurants, and theaters did their most thriving business on Friday nights and Saturdays. Minister Ishay has energetically attempted to revive and enforce these laws, to the great indignation of the secular community. He has sent an army of inspectors—usually Israeli Druze so as to avoid Jews' desecrating the Sabbath—out into the field armed with summonses and subpoenas for Jewish store owners whose businesses operate on the Sabbath. In one of the more dramatic cases in point, the court dealing with labor issues (Beit Din Le'avodah) imposed a large fine of 120,000 NIS (new Israeli shekels) on an offending business. In so doing, it was only being faithful to the letter of the written law. In 1998, the United Torah Judaism Party submitted a number of demands to Prime Minister Netanyahu central to which is enforcement of the Sabbath law. A secular riposte came in the form of a Tel Aviv municipal statute, which specifically permitted the opening of places of entertainment and culture on the Sabbath. For his part, the minister of the interior from the Shas Party has been delaying its implementation.[13]

But in practice, as noted, Ishay's campaign runs counter to the overwhelming sociocultural and economic tendencies that have transformed Israeli society in recent years. Israel has undergone a cultural sea change, an accelerated process of Westernization (more accurately, Americanization), which has had a decisive effect on how Israelis spend their leisure time, that is, the Sabbath and holidays. During the first generation of Israel's history, a Spartan simplicity marked its styles of recreation. Israel was a mobilized society, a society in the thrall of an ideological vision—not to mention a rather poor society—in which café life and the pleasures of the theater, not to speak of shopping excursions, were viewed somewhat askance. (For example, the town in which both authors resided when this text was written, Kfar Sava, did not have a single restaurant or café twenty-five years ago; today, there are probably forty.) Leisure time was spent either with family or in nature outings. The recreational options available in today's affluent environment have altered Israeli society deeply, perhaps even essentially. The strenuous hikes of the 1950s have been replaced by country clubs and spas, picnics by restaurants, and evenings of communal singing by bars and discos. For much of the young middle class, this is the only Israel they know.

Minister Ishay's campaign, aimed at enforcing the Sabbath laws that remain on the books, is perceived by secular Israel as a galling and sharply anachronistic crusade at fashioning the character of the Sabbath in congruence with Halacha and with Orthodox lifestyles. Israel's liberal, secular newspaper, *Ha'aretz*, has declared it outright: Ishay's campaign is an attempt to "transform Israel into an halachic state."[14] One can no longer speak of these struggles as local, specific, or marginal conflicts over the Sabbath, as was so often the case in the past. Sabbath days in early 1998 witness the regular transformation of Israel into one large area of contention. These struggles take place along all the major roads and at many of the important traffic junctions in Israel—from shopping centers at Bilu Junction (Negev) to the Tel Aviv greater metropolitan area (Shefa'im) to the lower Galilee (Gan Shmuel) to the north (Alonim). It is no surprise, then, that the press devotes a great deal of space on Sunday morning to the previous day's confrontations.[15]

The quality of discourse, its growing stridency and mutual derogation, accurately reflects this pitched battle between the camps. A single example will suffice. Yossi Sarid, leader of the secular, dovish Meretz Party, spoke to a crowd at one of the sites of conflict. He related the recent halachic decision of Rabbi Ovadiah Yosef (the venerated leader of the Shas Party), which prohibits picking one's nose on the Sabbath— a decision that had been ridiculed by many in the secular media.[16] Sarid declared, and Israeli radio carried his words, that he was prepared to enter into a compromise with Shas and its leader: "We won't pick our noses on the Sabbath and they won't stick their noses into our lives."[17] The sense of elation and high humor on the one side contrasted dramatically with the sense of deep mortification and offense on the other. For all of its tragicomic qualities, it was a revealing and increasingly typical moment in Israel's religious-secular conflict.

One student of the Haredi world described the major fear of the first generation of Haredi leaders as "erosion," that is, the anxiety that growing numbers of its young would desert the fold, enticed by secular temptations. The religious camp perceived itself as being on the defensive. Gradually, this sense of vulnerability and frailty has given way, first, to a sense of health and confidence and, more recently, to a frame of mind best described as triumphalist.[18] The sense of superiority to secular society is regularly proclaimed. The Haredim are the bearers of values and principles, in contrast with secular nihilism and loss of direction, and they promise true happiness and fulfillment, in contrast with secular neuroses, broken families, drugs, greed, and criminality.

This triumphalist logic was expressed first by the national religious community in the context of their religio-messianic drive to establish settlements in Judea and Samaria. Their sense of being the idealist pioneers of the 1970s and 1980s—having replaced the old Labor pioneers of the Yishuv era, whose sons and daughters had gone flabby with Westernized lifestyles—was the common coin of their discourse. As with so much else in the religious world, however, the Haredim have taken over in this regard from the national religious, as well.

Today, many Haredi leaders have no inhibitions about openly proclaiming their objective: to control Israel. After the stunning performance of Shas in the 1996 elections, for example, Rabbi Elbaz, one of the charismatic figures in the Shas Party, declared in celebration (carried live by Israeli TV, channel 1), "With the help of God we will transform the Knesset into a Beit Knesset," that is, a synagogue. In a confrontation that took place in the south—not an area notable in the past for Haredi influence or even physical presence—the spokesman of the Gerer Hasidim was quoted as declaring passionately: "We are all over Israel. . . . Our objective is to spread out all over the country in order to disseminate the word of Torah and to stop secular deterioration." The secular response did not tarry in coming. The mayor of a southern town proclaimed that he, as an army officer, had "undergone many battles" and he was "utterly determined to protect his town against the barbarians of the Gerer Hasidim." (It should be noted that the Gerer Hasidim are no marginal group; they are one of the largest and most powerful groups within the Haredi world.)[19]

These examples are only the anecdotal tip of a very real iceberg. In Tiberias, a secular family's car was fire-bombed by religious zealots for "offenses" they had committed. In Kiryat Gat, *mezuzot* were systematically torn off the doorposts of a religious community. In Neve Rotem, a Molotov cocktail was hurled at a mobile home used by Shas as community center and synagogue, and it went up in flames. The ultra-Orthodox on Bar-Ilan Street accumulated their infant's loaded diapers all week and, on the Sabbath, hurled them at the police, who were keeping the street open to traffic. In Ramat Gan, congregants were astounded to find pornographic photos plastered over the windows of their synagogue. Journalists pondering the likelihood of a Kulturkampf in Israel were assured by one of their colleagues that the issue was no longer relevant, because the war had already started.[20] Others described the secular-religious reality as the mouth of a volcano just before it erupts. The secular "revolt is near" they asserted; "we feel it coming to a boil."[21]

The ultra-Orthodox exemption from army service is a particularly potent example of these deteriorating relations. In secular eyes, it is perhaps the most infuriating of all grievances against the Haredim.[22] Part of the reason for this indignation lies, no doubt, in the fact that the national religious community, in contrast with the Haredim, has actively shouldered its security responsibilities, and they have expressed deep rancor at the Haredim for evading theirs. Moreover, Haredi coalitional leverage has, of late, led to a dramatic broadening of the exemption; the old yearly quotas were set aside, and the numbers of nonserving Haredim has risen precipitously. It has been widely reported, indeed, that the heads of the Haredi educational institutions do all they can to include all and sundry under the exemption—whether they are appropriate for advanced yeshiva study or not—in order to keep the young out of Zionist hands, as far as possible from the influence of the non-Haredi world. What is more, many of those exempted in order to continue their religious studies are reported (in government studies) to be doing anything but studying. No surprise, then, that the bitterest expressions of secular rage relate to this issue.

How intense these feelings of bitterness are can be adequately assessed only against the background of the growing percentages of secular young men and women who also do not serve in the army. It is a well-known although often bemoaned fact that the IDF is losing its character as a people's army. A larger population together with growing military professionalization have led to a substantial decline in the proportion of each year's potential recruits who are actually drafted and in the proportion of those drafted who actually complete their service. Moreover, the stigma and the economic disabilities that in the past came with avoiding the draft—once powerful deterrents—no longer carry with them the social opprobrium or the practical handicaps they once did. (Some analysts, in fact, applaud the idea of a professional military with a considerably reduced standing army and far less reliance on the mobilization of reserves.)[23] No less a figure than the IDF's head of personnel predicted that by the year 2000 only about 50 percent of potential draftees will, in fact, be conscripted. Some, like pop singer Aviv Geffen, after lauding draft evasion, have been lionized in some circles as cultural heroes. Considering this decline in the centrality of conscription in Israeli life, and in the numbers who actually do serve, it would have been expected that the intense reaction to Haredi nonservice would moderate over time. After all, their nonservice is congruous with the tendencies that are becoming dominant in the secular world, as well. Yet the issue of Haredi nonservice continues to be at the top of the secular agenda, a veritable red flag that regularly sets off paroxysms of anger. This anger is not limited specifically to nonservice alone: it tends to be the source of a blanket disqualification of Haredim in secular eyes.

Why this acuteness of passion? First of all, the numbers of Haredim with official exemptions seems to be clearly related to growing Haredi political leverage. Political power is being visibly exploited in order to exempt a certain defined community of young men—numbering today in the tens of thousands—from sharing in the most defining experience in the Israeli coming of age. With the Haredim it is not a question of deliberate IDF policy or of individual prevarication, as it is with the secular nonservers. Moreover, Haredi rationalizations for nonservice—to wit, "these young men kill themselves for the sake of Torah" (*meymitim et atzmam be'ohala shel Torah*)—are perfectly calculated to enrage those who risk real death on the battlefield.

Second, Haredi isolation from the Israeli collective, their tendency not to mix residentially, educationally, culturally, or commercially with non-Haredim, deny them the normal neighborly and social bonds that often moderate the animosities born of ideological and cultural distance. Third, Haredi men are brought up with the goal of spending all of their adult lives in Torah study. Being gainfully employed is considered a lesser form of Jewish life. In practice, living one's life in study means living at the public expense, being supported by all manner of government subventions the source of which are, of course, other Israeli taxpayers. With an entire community relying on government largesse, the need for political leverage to ensure its continuation grows apace. Hence, the dynamic of Haredi politicization: to ensure draft exemption and government budgets, they need to become politically more aggressive, but in so doing they earn the enmity of Israeli society at large.[24]

The core problem seems to be that the Haredim have become politically more ambitious and more aggressively intrusive, although they visibly disdain the society they seek to control. While collectively exempting themselves from the draft and isolating themselves from Israeli society, they are simultaneously determined to influence policy in regard to security and to have a decisive voice in fashioning the character of Israeli society. They protest territorial compromises or the dismantling of settlements while leaving to others—many of whom oppose these policies—the security burden these policies entail. They want to close the shopping malls on the Sabbath, although they are unlikely to shop there even on weekdays. It is here, in the incongruity between power and participation, that the rancor grows.

One interesting incident that combines many of these different sources of enmity took place in budget debates (in the context of growing unemployment and recession) in early 1998. The Haredim demanded that yeshiva students be given inexpensive, publically subsidized housing. The National Union of University Students reacted by going on strike. They complained that the Haredim and their yeshivot were being given unfair advantages. Haredim were being paid to study while secular students were being asked to pay more and more for a university education. Why the difference in treatment? They needed to work while studying in order to pay for tuition costs, while Haredim lived off the very taxes the secular students paid. They needed to search for housing (expensive and difficult to find), while the Haredim were going to be given apartments for next to nothing. The "parasites," as they described the Haredim, those who evaded their most basic national duty, military service, were being favored because of the politically strategic position of the ultra-Orthodox parties.[25]

To dramatize the injustice as they saw it, they staged a bitterly sarcastic variant on a classic military exercise: the stretcher-bearing march—a march with a stretcher carrying a (pretend) wounded soldier that is run at a murderous pace—in Hebrew, *masa alunkot*. In place of *alunkot,* or stretchers, however, they spoke of what they were doing as a *masa alukot* (*alukot,* "leeches" or "parasites"). On the stretcher was no wounded soldier but a traditional Haredi black hat. The message was clear: while students who engage in arduous and dangerous service for their country are forced to struggle to study, to make ends meet, and to find adequate housing, the Haredim who dodge the draft are showered with benefits by a government beholden to their political representatives.

How strident this enmity to Haredim can become must be anecdotally conveyed. In other contexts, this kind of demonization of the Haredim would be condemned as scurrilous anti-Semitic vulgarity. But in the atmosphere of the 1990s it passes without remark. "Tzitzim" (Tits), a popular sexual-political cabaret show, presents a scene in which an ultra-Orthodox man stands praying, his body gently swaying, his hands waving overhead beseeching heaven. A shapely women passes. The gentle swaying becomes jerky and libidinal, his hands are lowered into the folds of his black coat, and amidst cries of devotion and groans of ecstasy, the grisly scene comes to an end.

More recently, the popular TV program *Hachartzufim*—a political satire with puppets that represent the country's political leaders—presented the Haredim as sitting down to a festive meal in which the main course consisted of a secular Israeli; the Haredim argue vocally about who will drink the secular Israeli's blood, who will eat his fat. To be sure, afterward, some religious protests were lodged. Far more significant, however, is the apparent confidence of the program's producers that their audience is sympathetic to this kind of message.

From Crosscutting to Overlapping Cleavages: Religious Hawkishness versus Secular Dovishness

The transformation of the religious community, both in its national religious and Haredi segments, from a generally moderate and centrist force to one supporting hawkish, right-wing politics is one of the most dramatic developments in post-1967 Israeli politics. The catalysts and prime movers of this transformation were the second-generation national religious leadership, who refashioned the NRP into a party at the virtual right-wing margins of Israel's ideological spectrum. Gush Emunim, the flagship movement championing settlements and rejecting the Oslo process, was established in the 1970s by this same cohort from the national religious community. The ideological hard core as well as the demographic preponderance of committed settlers is identified unequivocally with the religious Zionist camp. Members of the national religious community were also among the founders of the right-wing Tehiya (Renaissance) Party, which was born in the early 1980s out of opposition to the Camp David accords. Nor is it any secret that many of the supporters and leaders of the Moledet Party—the most right-wing of Israel's parties—are from this same national religious constituency.[26] It was not, therefore, merely the Likud's rise to power in 1977 that upset the historical alliance between Labor and the NRP; the NRP itself was undergoing an accelerated process of reconstitution into a genuinely hawkish party.

In 1992, with the rise of the Rabin Labor government, this reconstitution was so advanced that the NRP could no longer sit in a coalition that contained Meretz, the dovish secular party that is very nearly its antithesis. Indeed, the NRP's campaign slogan—"The NRP at your right hand" (*Hamafdal le'yemincha*)—left little to the ideological imagination. In the 1996 election campaign, the NRP called upon its voters to support the Likud's Netanyahu, and, in fact, roughly 90 percent of the national religious constituency followed that advice.

During Netanyahu's prime ministership, the NRP stood out as the central defender of settlers, settlements, and noncompromise on the territorial issue. Interestingly, religious issues figured in its programs only secondarily, and when they did arise, they were presented with less passion or unconditionality than had accompanied the party's uncompromising opposition to the Oslo process. Moreover, the political hawkishness of the NRP was not likely to be altered by changing circumstances. As opposed to "security hawks," whose position depends upon a certain reading of the military value of the territories, Palestinian intentions, geopolitical realities, and the like—a position amenable to revision should reality evolve in new directions—the NRP's hawkishness rests upon principled religious-messianic-halachic imperatives. The halachic decrees of rabbinic authorities broadly associated with the NRP—to the effect that retreat from the "biblical homeland" was prohibited, even that religious soldiers must disobey orders rather than aid in the dismantling of settlements—were highly visible manifestations of this synthesis of religiosity and hawkishness. In other words, the NRP community does not consist of hawks who happen to be religious; their hawkishness is essentially religious in character.[27] Israel's sovereignty over the territories is, for them, inextricable from their collective self-understanding, from what they understand as the substance of Jewish religious and national identity.

Whatever the direct or secondary responsibility (if any) of this community for the assassination of Prime Minister Rabin, the public at large surely grasped the national religious identity of the assassin as anything but happenstance. It was the religious community that had spearheaded the vociferous demonstrations against Rabin's policies with their calls of "death to Rabin" and posters of Rabin in an SS uniform; it was from within this community that whispers and insinuations about Rabin being a *boged* (traitor), a *moser* (informer), a *rodef* (would-be murderer deserving of the death penalty) had emanated. This association of the violent radical right with the national religious community had also been prepared, inter alia, by the national religious character of the terrorist "Jewish underground" and by the similar provenance of Baruch Goldstein, the mass murderer at the Tomb of the Patriarchs in Hebron. Even before the assassination, the kinship between religious Zionism and zealous right-wing politics was a firm fixture in the Israeli public imagination.[28]

At the other end of the ideological continuum, a similar but mirror-imaging phenomenon was unfolding. Secularism and dovishness were also showing deep elective affinities for one another. Meretz was, as noted, the NRP's nemesis and antithesis; it compounded a systematically dovish position on security issues with a dogged opposition to the "illegitimate" influence of religious institutions in Israel's public life. Meretz's leader until 1996, Shulamit Aloni, was commonly identified as the voice of militant secularism and, simultaneously, as a leading champion of dovish positions in security and foreign policy issues. As early as 1970, she argued—then quite boldly—that the NRP's strategy was that of establishing a halachic state in Israel.[29] Hence, her appointment as minister of education and culture in the Rabin government of 1992 was nothing less than a red flag waved before the outraged religious community. Her highly controversial and abrasive statements on religious issues quickly plunged the coalition (which included the ultra-Orthodox Shas Party) into a serious crisis, which led Rabin to replace Aloni as minister of education.

Although not with the same insistence or system as the bond between religiosity and hawkishness, there are many on the left (and, of course, on the right) who also perceive the link between secularism and dovishness as inherent and necessary. A secular worldview, they explain, is liberated from the worship of "sand and stones," of thousand-year-old tombs, of xenophobic nationalism and tribal self-righteousness, of God-sanctioned violence. Secular thinking, because it is not burdened with absolutes and eternal truths, can be creative, pragmatic, and realistic. Moreover, a secular individual is, in fact, more likely to champion democratic norms than to defer to traditional authorities; hence, secular Israelis are more likely to adopt the view that governing a conquered and unwilling people constitutes an ongoing and grievous blow to Israel as a genuine democracy.

However these claims are assessed, there can be no doubt that on the ground, that is, among Israeli voters and political figures, these two pairs of loyalties—religiosity and hawkishness, secularism and dovishness—have increasingly become the fixed antipodes of Israeli politics.[30] The NRP and Meretz embody what is probably Israel's single most defining cleavage in its purest and most concentrated form. The religious-secular struggle more and more becomes identified with, even identical to, the conflict between hawks and doves. Although taken together the NRP and Meretz account for less than 20 percent of political representation in the Knesset, the antithesis they represent goes far beyond their institutional boundaries.

Although the Haredi camp's position is more complex than that of the NRP, it, too, has felt the force of the religious-secular polarization, which has swept them sharply rightward, as well. Although the Haredi parties—most conspicuously, Shas—are still available coalitionally to both large parties, the fit between them and the parties of the right has proven to be more congenial and sustainable. This is precisely what makes them scale-tipping parties. In 1990, for example, there was a readiness on the part of both Agudat Israel and Shas to join a Labor-led coalition. In 1992, Shas did in fact join the Rabin government. Moreover, and of potentially great significance, some of the Haredi leadership—against the preference of their followers—is of a distinctly dovish character.[31] Rabbi Ovadiah Yosef of Shas and Rabbi Menachem Schach of the Agudat Israel (formerly Degel Hatorah) are both noted for their tendency to prefer peace to territory.

Nevertheless, defining the Haredi camp by some of its individual leaders would badly distort the dramatic developments that have transformed it over the course of the past decade and a half. Today, the Haredi community at large has become a non-Zionist right wing of considerable passion—an unprecedented phenomenon in Israel. For example, Haredim voted for Netanyahu even more massively than did the national religious community—by most estimates, in the range of 95 to 97 percent; in some clearly defined Haredi areas, the vote was virtually 100 percent for Netanyahu. In Kfar Chabad (home of the Lubavitcher movement in Israel), for example, there was a virtually unanimous block vote for Netanyahu, and nearly 70 percent voted, in their second ballot, for the ultra-right-wing Moledet Party. As opposed to the national religious leadership that instructed its constituency to vote for Netanyahu, the Haredi parties desisted from any recommendation, not because they had none but because they feared that, in any case, their cohorts would vote for Netanyahu, whatever the counsel they offered.[32]

Many are the reasons for this transformation. Briefly and schematically, they derive from the Haredi sense of being overwhelmed by the growing Westernization and permissiveness of Israeli society, a development they associate with Israel's left wing. Nor can they fail to include the tendency of non-Haredi traditional Jews to be preponderately right-wing in their sympathies. Moreover, because of high birthrates, the old Haredi enclaves in Jerusalem and Bnei Brak are no longer able to house the very numerous new generation, and an outflow to various Haredi settlements in the territories has begun. Haredi towns in the West Bank have grown substantially in recent years. This, too, disposes the Haredi community to territorialist hawkishness. Even when the Haredi overflow stay within the "green line," their intrusion into areas that were formerly secular or mixed (that is, secular and national religious) in character has set off pitched battles in various locations all over the country. In these battles, the locals who resist Haredi incursion have been visibly supported by Israel's secular left-wing parties. It is no secret, of course, that calls for the drafting of Haredi young men derive preponderately from the left wing. It is also true that Likud voters are substantially more traditional than Labor Party voters. Some argue, in fact, that religious rhetoric, with its fraught historical associations and its uncompromising tenor, gravitates naturally toward right-wing themes. Taken together, these factors have catapulted the Haredi community, which, in the past, was often politically impassive, into the thick of right-wing politics.

Not only do Haredim participate in demonstrations against Sabbath desecration as they always have; they are also now visible in substantial numbers at political protests against the Oslo process. Being undeterred (as are the national religious) by historical ties with secular Zionism, by residential proximity with the nonreligious world, and by a long-term ideological engagement with democratic values, they constitute an aggressively formidable force on the right. Survey research makes plain how deep and how broad this Haredi commitment to hawkish politics has become. Indeed, gauged by some measures they outstrip the national religious community in this regard. All of this strengthens both the perception and the reality of a traditional-religious-hawkish bloc poised against a secular-dovish adversary.

Although less clearly delineated than the divide between the religious-

hawkish and the secular-dovish, another set of important sociodemo-
graphic attributes tends to correlate substantially with it, as well: the
Ashkenazi-Sephardi divide, together with the related issue of higher and
lower economic status. Being considerably more Westernized and less traditional than their Sephardi fellow citizens, Ashkenazi Jews tend to more
dovish positions. (Roughly seven of ten Sephardim vote for the right, and
a slightly lower number of Ashkenazim vote for the left.) Because Ashkenazim tend to be more advanced economically and in terms of educational attainments than Sephardim, this divide is exacerbated by class and
cultural resentments, as well. The resulting picture, although not always
sharp or orderly (the settlers are, for example, overwhelmingly Ashkenazi) is one in which hawkishness, religiosity, Sephardi origin, relatively
depressed economic status, and lower educational attainments constitute
one broad electoral-ideological constituency, and dovishness, secularity,
Ashkenazi origin, relatively comfortable economic status, and higher educational attainments form the other.

What is especially noteworthy in this divide is the specifically religio-
cultural way in which it tends to be expressed. Class issues per se—that
is, in the standard European form of lower-class espousal of socialist
egalitarianism of some sort juxtaposed with upper-class championing of
property rights—have only a faint echo in Israeli public life. Whether
this is because the language of class struggle adopted by pioneering socialist Zionism has become hopelessly archaic, or because narratives of
class struggle were preempted by Ashkenazi radicals and are, moreover,
culturally uncongenial to Sephardim, or because the broad overlap between class and ethnic lines favors an ethnocentric explanatory narra-
tive, the familiar discourse of class struggle is almost entirely absent in
Israel. In its place, there are charged communal images, cultural rallying
calls, and ethnic grievances. (Notably, the public spokespersons of what
are euphemistically called social issues are virtually all Sephardim.) In
other words, class issues tend to be transmuted into ethnocultural ones.

What stands out among these ethnocultural issues is the salience and
centrality of Jewish tradition and its religious resonances. It is no acci-
dent, of course, that the single Sephardi party in Israel, Shas, is an intensely religious one. Shas's remarkable electoral successes derive from
its ability to canalize social and economic grievances into an ethnoreli-
gious program. Indeed, Shas's central image, repeatedly used in its election campaigns, begins with a shofar blast at the Wailing Wall with the
words, "to restore the glory of yesteryear" *(le'hachzir atara le'yoshna)*

liturgically intoned in the background. Its venerated leader is not a politician but a rabbinic scholar whose authority is perceived as religious in character.

Nevertheless, it has been shown conclusively that the bulk of Shas voters are not ultra-Orthodox in their lifestyles; the majority are not even Orthodox-observant, if anything near rigorous definitions are applied.[33] Shas's constituency is heavily composed of Sephardi traditionals, largely from areas that are economically depressed and ethnically segregated—most notably, the so-called development towns. Ashkenazi culture with (what is seen as) its secular vacuousness and permissiveness, its Western orientations, its liberal humanism, its airs of cultural superiority, its unjust economic dominance, its sympathy for "progressive" and pluralist Judaism including the distasteful practices of the Conservatives and the Reform, and, of course, its tendency to "understand" the Arabs while traducing their own Jewish heritage are the oft-repeated themes of Shas's leadership. Religious resonances, in other words, are never far from ethnocultural grievances; and, for the most part, these religious motifs are popularly correlated with hawkish politics.

Although a host of caveats are in place, it is broadly true, nevertheless, that the ethnic, cultural, class, and educational cleavages that divide Israelis usually tend to coincide with the divisions dictated by religion and security affairs; they feed into rather than blur the divide between the religious-hawkish and the secular-dovish. Despite their individual uniqueness and irreducibility, these ethnocultural divides (which might have mitigated the secular-religious controversy), tend in fact to exacerbate many of the same hostilities and to underwrite many of the same political loyalties as the religious-secular divide.

It goes without saying that were the religious-secular divide sharply bounded—with the Orthodox on one side and the non-Orthodox on the other—the Orthodox would be overwhelmed by a roughly 80 percent non-Orthodox majority. This, however, is not the case. There is large-scale blurring at the point where religious politics and right-wing politics meet, a blurring that produces a virtually even split between the two camps in the Israeli electorate. The power of the right, beyond the 20 percent religious, is based mostly upon those many traditional, Sephardi, economically disadvantaged, and so forth for whom the Jewish nature of Israel is being threatened by the secular left and for whom the state's Jewish character is integrally associated with Judaism as a religious tradition. Simultaneously and complementarily, the perception that secular

dovishness derives from a deficient connection with the biblical homeland, that the left has little in the way of Jewish pride, that its willingness to concede and compromise is explained by its desire to enjoy Western affluence undisturbed by national responsibilities, these are typical
elements through which religious resonances link up with hawkish politics. Although, as noted above, the NRP and Meretz embody the archetypical examples of this, the master cleavage in contemporary Israeli politics, its central themes are reenacted and transposed onto other cleavage
lines, as well—each with its own unique ideological and cultural inflec-
tions.

Textbook political science tells us that when cleavages are parallel (or
overlapping) in the manner we have been describing, political crises are
not far off. When one can predict the political beliefs of an individual
just by a *kipah*, an accent, or an address; when one characteristic tends
to be systematically linked with a whole series of others; when grievances in one area connect to and aggravate grievances in another; when
cleavages cumulate rather than cut across and defuse each other, separate, often sealed sociocultural worlds are the result. Dialogue across
this multilayered divide, not to speak of actual accommodation, becomes difficult in the extreme.

But what of our argument in chapter 1 that consociational arrangements develop precisely when communal conflicts become unmanageable? Ostensibly, the more dangerous the cleavage, the more likely it is
that the familiar patterns of concession and accommodation will return.
Why, then, under these menacing circumstances, do the dynamics of consociational politics fail to assert themselves? At least two conditions need
to obtain for this to occur: First, the conflict needs to be essentially
sectarian, with each group aiming at the preservation of its own communal interests and distinctive character. Second, the leadership of the
various communities must have the political will to enter into such negotiations and the power to have the concessions they secure respected by
their own as well as by other contending communities.

These conditions do not obtain in contemporary Israeli public life.
Critically important is the total and categorical manner in which both
territorial and Jewish issues are currently perceived by the contending
socioideological camps. In regard to religious concerns, it is no longer a
matter of narrowly religious objectives such as closing a specific street
to traffic on the Sabbath, defining the Jewishness of this or that individual, determining the limits of the rabbinic courts' jurisdiction, or desig-

nating budget allocations to religious institutions. No longer are the familiar and circumscribed religion-state issues the heart of the matter. These are sectarian issues, that is, issues that relate to the basic needs of a particular community and can be, more or less, quarantined from, or at least made to appear compatible with, the practical functioning of society at large.

These are also the kinds of issues that are amenable to consociational arrangements. They are issues about how the pie is to be divided among its various claimants and, as such, can be negotiated to a workable settlement in which each side feels that its basic needs have been fairly addressed. Negotiations of this kind deliberately desist from posing questions about the essential nature of the political community, its fundamental character, direction, and purpose. There is broad agreement that because a plurality of communities must coexist with one another, any attempt to decide definitively about the ultimate character of the polity is precisely what must be avoided. Enduring consociational systems (Belgium and Switzerland come to mind) are based on the deeply internalized premise that there can be no such ultimate determination, that the basic identity of the polity does not transcend the plurality of groups that constitute it.

From a struggle over specific and, hence, resolvable religion-state issues, Israel at the turn of the millennium appears to be moving toward a principled and first-order struggle over the very nature of the Jewish state. A "politics of Jewish identity," it might be called. What kind of a political community will Israel be—one whose central loyalty is to the Jewish nation, its separate, enclavic integrality, its halachic and religious traditions, or one whose Jewish national character is mediated through the prism of modern, Western, and democratic values? These are, in their nature, ultimate and nonnegotiable (or at least nonresolvable) issues—a fortiori, when the contending sides perceive compromise as both irrelevant and insufferable.

The power of this cleavage was quite apparent in the 1996 elections. Whatever short-term factors may have contributed to Netanyahu's surprise victory, the electoral split along the "Jewish identity" line of cleavage is of cardinal importance. Although some two-thirds of Jewish Israelis reported supporting the Oslo process to one degree or another, about 55 percent voted for Netanyahu. Alongside the desire to slow down the Oslo process by much tougher bargaining, these election results need to be understood, we believe, at least as much as a victory of a "Jewish identity" coalition that saw in Peres-Beilin, Oslo, and Westernization looming threats to the Jewish character of the state. They voted for a candidate who would support "Jewish values" and preserve Israel in the traditional mold rather than for one who would scuttle the peace process—for a candidate who, as the campaign slogan had it, was "good for the Jews."

For some—especially those with NRP sympathies—the territorial issue is simply another aspect of Jewish identity. A genuinely Jewish Israel that relinquishes control over the national patrimony, over the biblical heartland, is a virtual contradiction in terms. Consociational concessions and deference in such circumstances make no more sense, they would contend, than bargaining with the Messiah or compromising over which of God's commandments ought to be fulfilled. Although others who flocked to the banner of Jewish identity did not necessarily fuse the two issues together so totally, the logic of their position was broadly analogous in principle, even if less rigorous in practice. A hard-line policy toward the Palestinians, inspired by "Jewish identity" concerns, a religiously nostalgic attitude toward the territories, admiration for the settlers who make great sacrifices for the sake of Jewish control of the holy places, all of these, to be sure, constitute a more loosely textured view than that of NRP stalwarts, but the basic fusion of Jewishness and hawkishness is there, nevertheless. With the lines of cleavage overlapping and reenforcing one another in this way, the prospects for consociational accommodation are none too good.

Consociational accommodation fails for another reason, as well. The territorial issue is perceived to be irreversible. Land that is relinquished is thought to be lost permanently; concessions made now will have to be lived with perpetually. Similarly, massive settlement activity carried out today will forever preclude retreat. Unlike most other security and foreign policy issues in the past, with their interim, *en procès* character, the territorial issue is being played for keeps: either a Palestinian state will be established in Gaza, Judea, and Samaria or the Jewish state will include these areas within its sovereignty. Neither at the level of principle nor at the level of political reality is there any perceived room for provisional solutions or halfway houses. Moreover, the loss of these areas to the Jewish state would mean, for many, a diminution of the state's Jewishness; it would signify the victory of pragmatism over Jewish ideals—the triumph of prosaic diplomacy and the abandonment of the singular Jewish historical calling.

The consociational strategy is effective when it is able to manage the normal distributions required in fluid political realities. It is a functional solution to ongoing functional problems. It ensures that no one wins big, but then again guarantees that no one loses big either. So long as the issues—however charged—are of the distributive, sectarian kind, consociational arrangements can take root. When, however, ultimate issues regarding a political community's first principles and physical borders are at stake, consociationalism loses its relevance and applicability. Under such circumstances, the logic of victory or defeat takes over.

Yitzchak Rabin recognized this truth when he embarked upon the Oslo peace process. Although his majority was tenuous, and (in his opponent's words) he even lacked a Jewish majority, he was undeterred in pursuing a highly controversial policy. Awaiting the rise of a united national front for peace or even endeavoring to present a peace plan broadly acceptable to Israeli society at large was, he understood, a recipe for paralysis. To pursue the peace process meant forgoing national unity and forging ahead in the face of very broad and very determined opposition. The choice was either to play to win or not to play at all. The ultimate nature of the questions at issue precluded strategies of a consociational variety. Much the same logic continues to prevail as the millennium draws to a close.

The basic correspondence between the issue of Jewish identity and the territorial issue, the perceived irreversibility of current decisions, the ultimate nature of the questions at stake are, in themselves, quite powerful deterrents to consociational accommodation. Add to them the dynamics of a balanced two-camp system, the enhanced power of the radicals in such circumstances, the ideological transformations that have radicalized the religious camp—all the factors dealt with in the earlier part of this chapter—and the grim prospects for consociationalism become quite apparent.

Nothing embodies this complex of anticonsociational factors as sharply and as repulsively as the assassination of Yitzchak Rabin. Yigal Amir's action took the logic of playing to win to its most gruesome conclusion. At the moment his gun fired, religious and territorial issues became indissolubly bonded with each other. The violent demonstrations that preceded the murder and the not insignificant number of cases in which it was lauded thereafter only reenforced the conviction that Amir was not a lone villain and that the fight over peace or territory had become a fight to the death.

Doubtless, there remain many at the center of the political spectrum for whom the old consociational style is still a beckoning option. These voices are not especially audible, however, in the political arena—certainly not in proportion to their numbers. The electoral dead heat between the contending camps and the resulting indispensability of the radicals on both sides tend to silence the moderate political center and to derail consociational efforts, even when they do manage to get started. Although the radicals may be a minority—albeit a substantial one—their strategic position magnifies their power, indeed, focuses the political system on the conflict as they perceive and conduct it.

There is a further necessary condition for consociational politics, and it, too, is lacking in contemporary Israel. Consociationalism requires clearly defined camps that are controlled by a leadership empowered to enter into agreements with rival camps. In the past, Mapai and the NRP represented such well-demarcated communal camps.[34] They not only represented the community's interests politically but, in addition, organized the lives of its constituents in many areas such as labor unions, banking services, newspapers, health care, welfare benefits, sports leagues, youth movements, housing, and the like. Control of these many communal services provided the party leadership with a commanding and decisive position in relation to party stalwarts. Indeed, it was the idea of one organized community negotiating, through its authorized leadership, with another similarly organized and led community that provided consociational arrangements with their distinctive logic and their peculiar force.

Nonreligious parties, both on the right and left, gradually lost their organized "camp" quality—today only faint suggestions of this dense party-centered support system endure. Although some of the familiar political code words are still heard, their political import has long been forgotten. For example, the names of Israel's soccer teams still betray their ideological origins—Ha'Poel Tel Aviv, Betar Jerusalem, Macabee Haifa—but their connections to politics have become quite tenuous. In their place a rich and diffuse civil society has emerged.[35] Thousands of new independent organizations provide the services once dispensed by the party apparatus, just as those party organizations that managed to survive the transformation lost their political coloration and became increasingly professionalized.

It took somewhat longer for the NRP to lose its camp qualities; today, however, this process is well advanced. With the loss of its consolidated camp character, the religious Zionist constituency no longer can be spoken of as a unified bloc. It does not routinely defer to the NRP leadership. Having become a sharply ideological party, as opposed to the aggregative communal representative it once was, the NRP has lost its ecumenical qualities; only those that subscribe to the message, approve the tactics, and esteem the leadership continue to be loyal members. Religious Zionists no longer vote for the NRP as a matter of course; they scatter their support among a wide range of parties. Not surprisingly, there have been spin-off parties to the NRP's right and left (Matzad and Meimad) as well as religious Zionist formations within other political parties.

Indicative of this breakdown of camps is the proliferation of nonparty political organizations that pursue independent agendas and policies. Today, it is not only parties that express political positions, arrange demonstrations, and lobby the government. Gush Emunim (Bloc of the Faithful), Shalom Achshav (Peace Now), Zo Arzenu (This Is Our Land), Dor Shalem Doresh Shalom (An Entire Generation Demands Peace), Va'ad Rabanei Yesha (Committee of Yesha [acronym for Judea, Samaria, and Gaza] Rabbis), and Am Chofshee (A Free People) represent only a fraction of the better-known organizations. With both of the main consociational actors lacking a consolidated camp upon which to rely, even if consociational negotiations could be initiated, the respective leadership would be hard pressed to discipline their widely scattered troops into accepting their agreements—all the more so, of course, if the concessions they granted their political rivals were substantial.

Only the Haredi parties retain the familiar patterns of a camp organization. Shas, most conspicuously of all, has, in a very short period, constructed an extensive network of educational and social services. Yet in the context of Israeli cultural conflict, Shas's camp character does not support consociational arrangements (even if a secular partner to the negotiations could be found). On the contrary, Shas's grassroots activities are quite distressing to secular Israel. For in contrast with the familiar (and legitimate) form of camp party that responds to its community's needs and interests with appropriate services and demands (and is, hence, amenable to consociational agreements), Shas's explicit objective is to missionize and grow, to energetically expand into non-Haredi, even non-Orthodox, populations. That it does this by offering welfare and educational services to what is often the most vulnerable socioeconomic stratum of society only fires secular indignation and alarm. Shas's communal services, in other words, are perceived not as the circumscribed, sectarian efforts of a distinct community but as proof of an aggressively imperialistic strategy. It is, in secular eyes, yet another attempt on the part of the religious to control the essential character of the entire political community. As such, Shas's camp character practically aggravates rather than potentially mitigates the secular-religious cleavage.

One central Sephardi member of the Knesset—Meyer Shitrit, leader of the Likud's parliamentary delegation and candidate to replace Netanyahu as its leader—expressed the fear that unless something is done to stop these tendencies now, the students of today "will wear *kaputot* [the Haredi long black coat] in twenty years." The former minister of the treasury (under the Labor Party), Beige Shochat, ventured even more dire predictions: "In less than ten years there is liable to arise here a Khoumeini-like state."[36] Shitrit and Shochat, it should be recalled, are anything but secular militants in the style of Shulamit Aloni; both belong to the moderate, centrist wings of their respective parties—which is to say that their fears are not wildly eccentric or atypical.

The May 1999 elections for prime minister and for the Fifteenth Knesset—as well as the process of coalition formation by Ehud Barak—constitute the temporal boundaries of our book. In the election's wake, we ought to assess, if only briefly and preliminarily, the current status of consociational politics.

On the one hand, the composition of the Fifteenth Knesset can only lead us to pessimism. It seems to verify our worst fears about the growing fractiousness and irresolvability of the religion-state issue. We seem to be reaping the Kulturkampf harvest of the seeds of anticonsociationalism we have sown. The Haredi parties, Torah Judaism and Shas, achieved an unprecedented twenty-two seats in the Knesset. (By comparison, in the Fourteenth Knesset they had fourteen.) The Haredi parties grew as the National Religious Party lost almost half its parliamentary representation (from nine seats to five). Only about 20 percent of the religious representatives in the Knesset (numbering twenty-seven) are non-Haredi—which goes a long way toward verifying our contention that there has been a changing of the guard in the Israeli religious world. It is clearly no longer the Zionist, army-serving, socially integrated NRP that represents religious interest in the public sphere. It is now the Haredim who have taken on the mantle of religious leadership—with all the anticonsociational, crisis-provoking consequences discussed earlier.

It should be added that although Torah Judaism joined the coalition, it did not accept any ministerial posts, and it is not difficult to foresee its abandoning the government if its religious sensibilities are offended. In such circumstances, Shas will find it difficult to maintain its loyalty to the coalition.

The struggle over the rule of law reached unprecedented heights during the election campaign. In the context of Deri's guilty verdict, Shas brutally attacked the law enforcement institutions as well as the court system; on the other hand, the secular parties made the issue of legality and governmental propriety the very heart of their message. The Ministry of the Interior, which for forty years (since the "Who is a Jew?" issue) had been controlled by religious parties, was now—after a bruising campaign battle—given to Israel Be'aliya.

Equal and opposite to the Haredi camp, there is now an ideologically militant secular camp that goes far beyond the bounds of traditional left-wing politics. In addition to Meretz, the veteran standard bearer of Western cosmopolitanism and secular values, we need to mention Shinui, sundry members of One Israel, like Ya'el Dayan, Roni Milo from the Center Party, and the Israel Be'aliya Party. (The latter's antireligious animus is addressed in chapter 5.) Shinui's success is perhaps the hottest news to have come out of the election. A splinter faction of Meretz, it was given up for dead by most political analysts. But in a deft stroke, Tommy Lapid, a journalist and TV personality well known for his strident and coarsely populist style as well as for his centrist-right politics, was drafted to lead the revitalized party under a belligerent, no-holds-barred anti-Haredi banner. He sweepingly rejected any cooperation with the Haredim and pledged not to serve in any government with a Haredi component. Clearly tapping a rich and festering reservoir of resentment, Shinui went from zero seats in the polls to six (that is, about 170,000 votes) in a matter of days. If ever there was a measure of how deep anti-Haredi feeling went, this was it. When the election results were announced, Meretz joined Shinui in its categorical rejection of cooperation with Shas. Meretz's resistance weakened rather quickly;[37] but Shinui, true to its word, refused to join the government. With Shinui acting as critic and competitor at Meretz's secular flank, the latter will surely feel itself limited in the kinds of concessions it can make in religious issues. This does not bode well for consociationalism.

An overview of the Knesset reveals that more than a third of its members manifest strong pro-Haredi or anti-Haredi sentiments. Extreme positions in this regard are today considerably more prevalent and bitter than in any previous Knesset. The consociational voices that remain will find it that much more difficult to get a serious hearing for their complex and conciliatory proposals. Judged by its composition, then, the Knesset seems poised to raise the crisis-dominated style to new levels of vehemence.

Nevertheless, the coalition that Ehud Barak put together after long and arduous negotiations is remarkably consociational in character. The coalition is wide—wider than it needs to be in terms of simple arithmetic calculations; it includes right- and left-wing parties as well as religious and secular parties. In theory, at least, cooperation in running governmental affairs offers the potential for mutual respect and feelings of partnership. The two large "antipodal" parties, Meretz and Shas, were well rewarded by Barak in terms of ministerial posts and government influence, which will make it harder for them to abandon the coalition: the price of leaving will be prohibitively high.

What is more, common anticipation of progress in the peace accords with both the Palestinians and the Syrians—issues in which the differences between Shas and Meretz are not insurmountable—is one of the mainstays of Barak's government. Barak has made it clear that critical decisions such as these need to be supported by a wide consensual rather than a narrow government. There is some likelihood that with issues of such gravity on the table, secular-religious battles will be temporarily suspended.

Some likelihood perhaps, but it is quite improbable that these incendiary religious-secular concerns can await the full completion of the peace process—a long, drawn-out affair according to the most optimistic appraisals. There are many issues urgently awaiting resolution: the status of the Conservative and Reform movements and related conversion concerns, the very large number of halachically non-Jews among the immigrants from the former Soviet Union, the exemption of yeshiva students from army service, Sabbath prohibitions enforced by Eli Ishay, the current leader of Shas, and so on.

This book is wary of predictions. Still, we feel no trepidation in foretelling that by the time it makes its way to bookstore shelves, many a secular-religious crisis will have rocked the government. How the various actors will respond to these crises is far harder to anticipate.

Chapter Four

The Judicial and Constitutional Dimension

This chapter takes up the judicial and legal aspects of consociation-alism's decline. It explores the effects of a formal written constitution on the politics of accommodation. The Israeli Supreme Court's tendency toward judicial activism is taken up, together with the constitutional revolution occasioned by the new Basic Law on Human Freedom and Dignity and Basic Law on Freedom of Occupation. Finally, the Basic Law on Government, which instituted the direct election of the prime minister, will be assessed in terms of its effects on the consociational style of politics.

Introduction: The "Judicialization" of Political Conflict in Consociational Democracies

A written, formal constitution would seem, prima facie, to accord with the consociational style of politics. After all, constitutions protect minority rights against the excesses of majoritarian rule. The supremacy of the constitution and the difficulties involved in changing its provisions ensure minorities that majority rule will stop short of trampling their essential interests and entitlements.

Arend Lijphart counts the presence of a constitution as one of the characteristics of "consensual" democracy. Consensual democracies, such as Switzerland and Belgium, differ from the consociational model in that they incorporate intercommunal agreements and their structural arrangements in formal constitutional documents. These arrangements are, therefore, governed by rigorous and principled legal standards.

Consociational models like Israel, by contrast, are neither notably vir-
tuous in character nor in line with the high standards of good gover-
nance. Many such morally and procedurally dubious deals aimed at defusing communal conflict were informally hammered out in the early
years of Israeli statehood.

"Judicializing" political conflict, that is, bringing intractable public
issues to the arbitration of the court, would seem, at first blush at least,
to run athwart of the consociational style. The judicial branch, by its very
nature, normally provides clear answers to the questions it adjudicates.
The dynamics of legal thinking do not center on finding an optimal compromise between rival claims, on leaving all parties to the dispute reasonably satisfied. The bargaining, deal-centered, accommodationist style
is foreign to judicial deliberations. Court cases end with decisions, not
with interest-driven armistices.

Nonetheless, it is often remarked that transferring thorny political
conflicts to the judiciary does have consociational benefits. One writer
notes that judicial decisions, given their aura of impartiality and profes-
sionalism, can "cool political passions and put an end to intense and long-
standing political conflicts." For example, the Israeli Supreme Court's
decision to allow television broadcasts on the Sabbath despite religious
opposition resolved a problem that might otherwise have become politically intractable.[1]

Why do judicial decisions succeed in managing conflict where politics
fail? As hinted above, the answer with respect to Israel lies in the high
prestige accorded to the Supreme Court and its judges. Many surveys
and much research consistently indicate that the Supreme Court is held
in high esteem by Israeli citizens, even when compared with high tri-
bunals in other Western democracies.[2] The image of neutrality and fairness that cling to the judicial system render it easier for the protagonists
to accept from the courts, and especially the Supreme Court (sometimes,
to be sure, with a gnashing of teeth), what they would not accept from
the more political branches of government. Politicians, too, will at times
divert to the courts issues that cannot be resolved politically. After an
authoritative judicial decision, they feel at least reasonably immune from
criticism within their own camp.

This is not to say, of course, that the various political camps will
accept any decision just because it comes from the courts rather than
from the political system. In regard to issues of high principle, decisive
win-or-lose court decisions can deal serious blows to the consociational

style of conflict management. In such cases, the injured party will some-times attempt to use its political leverage to nullify the decision by leg-islatively overriding the court's judgment. This is precisely what hap-pened in the well-known Shalit case. Benjamin Shalit, it will be recalled, an officer in the IDF, appealed to the Supreme Court to compel the Min-istry of the Interior to register his children as Jews despite the fact that their mother was not a Jew. The Supreme Court decided in his favor. This verdict crossed all the "red lines" of the religious camp—that is, it was simply intolerable to them.[3]

The court's decision relied on the absence of any clear legal specifica-tion of who is a Jew. Ironically, the absence of distinct criteria for Jew-ishness was part of the accommodationist style associated with conso-ciationalism. Consociationally, defining Jewishness was an issue too hot to handle, and it was left in a state of creative confusion by the various political camps. The court could, therefore, rely on popular rather than religious perceptions of who is a Jew. But this was not the last word on the subject. Spurred on by the religious parties, the Knesset in 1970 changed the Law of Return in a manner that disqualified the Jewishness of Shalit's children. Henceforth, a Jew would be understood as someone who was born of a Jewish mother or who had converted—a definition that, for the time being at least, placated Orthodox desires.

Judicializing political issues can foster consociational accommoda-tion when two conditions hold: The first is that judicial determinations are limited in scope, not directed at the most central conflict issues, and used sparingly. If, on the other hand, the courts understand their man-date as far reaching, if judicialization becomes the normal means of dealing with explosive political issues, and if the issues dealt with are primary and essential, the courts will quickly lose their erstwhile pres-tige and neutrality and become simply another protagonist on the polit-ical battlefield. The arrogation of such a role by the courts means, in effect, that consociational accommodation has given way to the decisive resolution of political controversy; and it is highly unlikely that the los-ing side will accept such judicial determinations with either resignation or equanimity.

The second condition is that the courts continue to be perceived as professional and nonpartisan rather than as a side to the conflict. If, on the other hand, the courts are viewed as ideologically determinate, that is, as partial to one side to the conflict—in our case, as we shall see, to the liberal Western as opposed to the Jewish and religious perspective—

the likelihood that its decisions will set politically charged conflicts to rest is severely undermined.

The discussion below focuses on three cardinal changes that have transformed the judicial and constitutional character of Israel, and they are taken up in chronological order. First, we consider the judicial activism practiced by the Supreme Court since the early 1980s. Second, we focus on the constitutional revolution that occurred in the early 1990s, when the Basic Laws on Human Freedom and Dignity and on Freedom of Occupation were passed by the Knesset. Third, we take up the implications for consociationalism of the Basic Law on the Government, with its central provision for the direct election of the prime minister. We contend that all three of these judicial and constitutional changes weaken the consociational style and foster a majoritarian, decisiveness-centered, and crisis-dominated style of Israeli politics.

Judicial Activism: The Broadening of Judicial Intervention

Judicial activism is a concept of American origin. The term is commonly used to describe the tendency of certain American Supreme Court justices to see their role vis-à-vis the legislature and the executive as initiating and assertive; in practice, this means they have little hesitation in disqualifying laws they feel are inconsistent with the Constitution. In the Israeli context, *judicial activism* has a somewhat different and broader connotation. Until the passage, in the early 1990s, of the Basic Laws guaranteeing various human freedoms, the ability to strike down Knesset laws was very limited, indeed. Nonetheless, the origins of Israeli judicial activism predate these Basic Laws by roughly a decade and are considerably broader than what is called "judicial review."

When the Basic Laws were passed, the Supreme Court was already sufficiently activist to seize upon them to both justify and further their assertive program. The activist program included vigorous court intervention into the judgments, procedures, decisions, and policies of the Knesset and the executive. In a series of appeals, beginning in the early 1980s, the Supreme Court intervened in the decisions of the Knesset and its various constitutive institutions. The height of this intervention came when the court actually nullified a decision of the Knesset's plenum—the body that, in the absence of a constitution, is often described as the ultimate repository of Israel's sovereignty.[4]

Another important aspect of activism is the decline of judicial formalism and its replacement by an approach that is clearly and unashamedly value directed. This approach has been described as "placing value restrictions on [Israeli] society and its organs of government . . . in an attempt to restrain the process of decline in values which affects all areas of life."[5] The controversy between judicial activism and judicial restraint is largely one that exercises the community of jurists.[6] Yet its practical effects are highly relevant for the struggle over the collective identity of the Jewish state.

One of the central arrangements hammered out during the formative period of Israel's consociationalism was the legal and authoritative status of the rabbinic courts. In this context, it was decided that marriage and divorce would follow Halacha and be performed under rabbinic aegis. This arrangement created an unparalleled judicial reality: two legal hierarchies existed side by side and operated with different legal codes. That they often found themselves in conflict with each other will come as no surprise. The extent of rabbinic authority and its ultimate subordination to the civil authorities were the most frequent sources of friction.

The confrontation between them reached its height in what is known as the *Bavli* decision, which serves as a cardinal example of judicial activism.[7] It began with a decision of the rabbinic court in the context of a divorce case. The rabbis rejected the divorcing woman's demand that the judicial proceedings related to financial arrangements between the couple be conducted according to civil rather than religious law. (It needs to be mentioned, if only parenthetically, that the woman's position is often stronger in civil rather than in religious law because the latter does not recognize the joint possession of property, as the former does.) In rejecting the woman's demand, the rabbinic court emphasized that the legal system of the civil courts "does not in any way obligate the rabbinic courts" and that the rabbinic courts "judge cases according to Jewish law in which the concept of joint ownership does not exist."[8] The woman appealed to the Supreme Court, which found in her favor.

The public storm that followed the decision related not only to the substance of the Supreme Court decision but also, and perhaps even more heatedly, to the justifications for the decision as formulated by Aharon Barak, the chief justice. Barak observes at the end of his decision that "I could have ended my decision here," that is, he could simply have found for the woman and left it at that.[9] If Barak had opted for this strategy, the *Bavli* case would have become just another in a rather long series of predictable confrontations between the two coexisting legal hierarchies—a reality with which the consociational style had long ago learned to live.

Barak did not opt for this strategy, however, and went on to clearly enunciate the principles upon which his decision rested. He concedes that the right of the rabbinic courts to deal, in halachic fashion, with civil issues that arise out of cases such as *Bavli* has some precedent in juridical literature; indeed, it is even "expressed in a number of Supreme Court pronouncements." Barak goes on to dismiss these precedents and pronouncements as "casual utterances" that are "fundamentally in error, and that should be abandoned."[10] His controversial conclusion was that in civil matters the rabbinic courts need to decide according to civil laws. In this case, to wit, the financial division between the divorcing couple, the rabbinic courts are obliged to accept the woman's contention and decide "according to general civil law." Barak, in his highly activist style, had decided to contravene accepted judicial practice and to make clear his own legal agenda.[11]

How contentious Barak's remarks were can be sensed quite strikingly in the dissenting opinion of Justice Menachem Alon, himself a religious Jew who was the court's expert in Jewish law and a consistent supporter of judicial restraint. Alon's cynicism is unrestrained. He says of Barak's activism,

[The Basic Law on] the Dignity of Law and Its Interpretation; [the Basic Law on] the Dignity of the Judge and His Interpretations. All settled then. A new revolutionary doctrine has come to the world. And, as is the way of revolutions, its weaponry is of the unconventional kind. Previous decisions and statements become casual utterances. And as if this did not suffice, they are also fundamentally wrong and should be abandoned. Let the preserver of law distance himself from them![12]

Alon's cynicism is mild, however, in comparison with the reactions of the judges in the rabbinic court system and the Chief Rabbis. Their hostile responses related both to the attempt to dictate to the rabbinic courts what they ought to be doing in their own courtrooms and to the content of his concluding remarks, the upshot of which were the obligation of the rabbinic courts to abandon halachic considerations and to decide according to the secular civil code of law.

It must be emphasized that this is but one example among many. Taken as a whole, the body of examples creates the impression—particularly in the religious community—that the court is of the liberal West-

ern persuasion and, what is more, fundamentally antireligious in its decisions. This impression was only strengthened by the decision of the
Supreme Court to recognize the partner of a homosexual steward working for El Al airlines as his spouse for the purpose of receiving spousal
benefits from the airline.

The willingness of the Barak court to assert its views, even though
they depart substantially from the precedents of the past, is only one—
and not necessarily the most important—aspect of judicial activism. The
extent of the court's authority, that is, the scope of what is judiciable, is
a serious source of friction, as well. There are, in fact, two different
issues at stake here. First is the principled question: Are all subjects and
domains judiciable, or are there areas from which the judiciary is fundamentally barred? Second, even if the answer to the first question is
that, in principle, there are no nonjudiciable areas, is it wise and appropriate for the court to intervene into all domains of individual, social,
and political life? These two questions are referred to in legal parlance
as "normative judiciability" and "institutional judiciability," respectively.
Barak has taken a consistently radical position in both regards. As to normative judiciability, he asserts that "law fills the land in its entirety" and
that "every controversy—even the most political of them—is judiciable."
Moreover, Barak argues, "from an institutional point of view, most controversies—including those of a political character—are judiciable."[13]

The court has also taken an outspoken position on the issue of "reasonableness" *(sveerut)*, to wit: how "unreasonable" must an action of
another branch of government be to justify judicial intervention? Barak
admits that "the choice between a number of reasonable options is a
decision that should be left to the governmental bodies themselves and
does not warrant judicial intervention." Nevertheless, he places great
emphasis on the "range of reasonableness" that sets the boundaries between governmental autonomy and judicial intervention.[14] The judiciary
is obliged to intervene in cases in which a branch of government over-
steps this boundary in a blatant way. If, Barak concludes, the court becomes convinced that the government action in question suffers from
extreme unreasonableness, it will not hesitate to nullify it outright. This
new assertive mood has the effect of opening the court's doors to appellants who have no clear personal standing or interest in the case and
can show no personal injury deriving therefrom. How this will affect the
boundaries between the various branches of government and the place
of the Supreme Court in the governmental mosaic is yet to be determined.

The practical consequences deriving from these aspects of judicial activism are especially well represented in the struggles over the exemption of yeshiva students from army service. We have dealt at length with the context and motives for the consociational accommodations that were involved in configuring the contours of this thorny issue. Because the draft of yeshiva students was understood to be a "red line" for the Haredi community, the majority of the justices abstained from compelling them to serve, even though the arrangement was nowhere established in a central legal precept but was based only upon a technical provision of the Security Service Law.[15]

Over the years, many have expressed deep dissatisfaction with this arrangement. Against this background, an appeal was filed with the Supreme Court in 1981 asking the court to compel yeshiva students to serve in the army like all other Israeli citizens. The appeal was rejected; but for our purposes what is of special interest here is the reasoning of the court—the court, it should be recalled, *before* the era of judicial activism. Justice Yitzchak Cohen spoke for the court:

The question of whether to draft yeshiva students or not is fundamentally a public problem, the solution to which ought to be left to those political actors whose role it is to decide in this matter. . . . What stands out in the appeal is the desire to drag this court into a sensitive and stormy political controversy. . . . The appellants will not succeed in doing so because they neither have any standing in this case, nor is the issue judiciable, nor have they succeeded in presenting a reason for the court's intervention.[16]

In this short passage, all the complementary elements of judicial restraint are clearly present: (1) the court does not deal with sensitive political issues; (2) it recognizes large areas of public life as nonjudiciable; and (3) it will not deal with individuals who have no real personal standing in the case.

In 1986, another appeal, relating once again to the drafting of yeshiva students, was brought before the court, this time against the background of its growing activism. The court rejected this appeal as well, but the changes in the court's reasoning are quite dramatic. This decision essentially reverses, at the level of principle, the fundamental axioms that underlay Justice Yitzchak Cohen's decision of some five years earlier. Justice Barak asserts, first of all, that the appellants do have standing before the court, even though they are not directly or personally affected by the nonservice of yeshiva students. What is more, he contends, "in this

appeal the principle of 'institutional nonjudiciability' does not apply,"
which means, in effect, that what was considered an overly political issue
into which the court would not intervene is now seen as fully within the
court's jurisdiction. Nevertheless, the court rejected the appeal on the
grounds that the judgments and evaluations of the other branches of government in this matter were not overtly unreasonable.

All the judges sitting in this case insisted upon the right of the court
to exercise its discretion, its sense of substantive justice, in issues such as
this. Thus, Meyer Shamgar, then chief justice, in giving the benefit of the
doubt to government policy, nonetheless described the nonservice of
yeshiva students as "unreasonable" and "unsatisfactory." Justice Miriam
Ben Porat (later to become the state comptroller) stressed that "it may
well be that in the future the proportions of those granted military deferments will reach such magnitude so as to become an important factor in
determining the reasonableness of the defense minister's approach, even
justifying the intervention of this court."[17]

It was clear from the activist decision in the 1986 case that yet another
appeal was only a matter of time. Indeed, a decade later, after Netanyahu
had formed his government and the tensions between the religious and
secular communities rose to unprecedented levels, the stage was set for
yet another judicial battle. In this case, there is no mistaking consociationalism's decline and the rise of a confrontationist style in Israeli public life. Notably, the appellants relied on the court's 1986 decision and
its promise to intervene if the deferments reached unreasonable levels.
Just this had happened, they claimed: there had been a sharp increase in
the number of those deferred because of yeshiva study, and this warranted court intervention. The entire arrangement, the appellants contended, needed to be fundamentally reassessed.[18]

All sides to the litigation were very much aware that this time the court
might actually accept the appeal and decide, in one fashion or another,
to strike down, or at least limit, the current arrangement. It was this wor-
risome prospect that prompted Netanyahu to establish a public committee to deal with the subject. Such a committee, it was thought, might
well serve as a justification for the postponement of court proceedings
until the committee had completed its work and made its recommendations.

The leadership of the Haredi community made its uncompromising
position as plain as it could. Rabbi Menachem Schach (the spiritual
leader of the Lithuanian branch of the Haredi world) declared simply

that "it is forbidden [for yeshiva students] to be drafted into the army—even if the price is sacrificing one's life." This is a case, Rabbi Schach continued, in which, halachically, one must "be killed rather than transgress." All the leaders of the Haredi world united behind this stand.[19]

The secular leadership responded in kind. Naomi Chazan, Knesset member from the Meretz Party, demanded that the attorney general begin an investigation of Rabbi Schach on the grounds that he had incited his people to rebellion.[20] Ehud Barak, the freshly elected leader of the Labor Party, circulated a petition calling for the drafting of Haredim. This was merely a preliminary step on the way to a law, proposed by Barak, that would nullify the current arrangement and make exemptions from service far more difficult to come by. The fact that a candidate for prime minister with uncertain popular support was willing to challenge the Haredim so overtly, that he was, moreover, so confident of massive backing for such a confrontationist move, speaks volumes for the decline of consociationalism.

Representatives of the Haredi community made it clear that they were not prepared to consider a compromise, not even in the form of the investigatory committee set up by Netanyahu. Knesset member Meyer Porush of the United Torah Judaism Party (Yahadut Hatorah Hameuchedet) threatened to leave the coalition if such a committee were allowed to operate. This forced Netanyahu's hand, and the committee was disbanded even before the ink on the document creating it had dried. "The crisis has ended," one journalist cynically remarked, but only "until the next time, and it will be soon."[21]

The so-called Conversion Law (Chok Ha'hamara) provides another telling illustration of the Supreme Court's growing activist posture. The prevailing understanding in regard to conversions has long been that Conservative and Reform conversions performed abroad would be recognized by the Ministry of the Interior for the purpose of population registry. In regard to conversion within Israel itself, by contrast, the Orthodox monopoly would be preserved. The non-Orthodox movements, whose power in Israel is meager, appealed to the Supreme Court to have their Israeli conversions recognized by the Ministry of the Interior. In effect, the Conservative and Reform movements were asking the court to break the Orthodox monopoly in religious matters, generally, and to validate non-Orthodox conversions, specifically.

It should be stressed that it was common knowledge on all sides to the controversy that this time there was a very good chance the court

would find for the non-Orthodox appellants and against the arrangements and practices that had prevailed until then. Precisely these prog-
noses led to the establishment of a committee led by Ya'acov Ne'eman,
minister of the treasury in the Netanyahu government, which included
among its members representatives from all of the religious movements.
As in the case of deferments from army service, it was thought that establishing a public committee to deal with the issue would keep the courts
at bay—temporarily, at least.

The Ne'eman Commission recommended that a conversion institute
common to all three movements be established while the actual conversion be Orthodox in character. This proposal was stillborn because of
the vociferous opposition of the Haredim, the Chief Rabbis, and the preponderance of the rabbinical establishment in Israel. When it became
clear that the Ne'eman Commission's recommendations were dead, the
non-Orthodox streams renewed their appeal to the Supreme Court, an
action that, inevitably, set off another round of stormy public debates.
Fearing a court decision they could not live with, the religious parties
renewed their demand that the prevailing arrangement, whereby Orthodoxy has exclusive control over conversion in Israel, be anchored in primary legislation rather than in technical provisions or nonbinding political understandings. Such legislation was specifically and deliberately
aimed at limiting the power of the Supreme Court. As with military service for yeshiva students, the last word on this subject is yet to be heard.[22]

Nothing that has been said is meant to give the impression that the
Supreme Court is the only, or even the main, body that raises controversial issues such as the nonservice of yeshiva students, conversion, and
the like. In fact, these issues dominate the public agenda again and again
because of the intensity inherent in struggles over the collective identity.
The courts constitute only one significant element in the failure of Israeli
consociationalism.

To be sure, there are a number of reasons for the court's particular
salience in secular-religious strife. First, the courts substantially limit
the free-wheeling ability of politicians to strike bargains and deals that,
whatever their propriety, defuse the charged nature of religious conflict.
The kinds of dubious arrangements that lubricated the wheels of government in the first decades of statehood are difficult to sustain when the
courts (as well as other bodies) carefully scrutinize political behavior and
impose liberal Western standards. Second, the courts have become an
institution of last resort for a growing number of secular Israelis who

despair of having their views adequately expressed in political life. In issues such as the exemption of yeshiva students from army service, for example, the Supreme Court has served as an essential conduit for opposition to what is perceived to be an intolerable injustice.

Third, the publicity that surrounds Supreme Court decisions ensures that the issues involved will become highly visible, that is, central to Israel's public agenda. The more an issue becomes a public matter of principle, the more likely that the contending sides will lock themselves into all-or-nothing positions, and conversely, the more difficult it becomes to find cool-headed compromise solutions. Fourth, in cases where Supreme Court decisions disqualify a prevailing practice, it will often prompt the losing side to overcome the court's opposition by anchoring the rejected practice in primary legislation. Such legislative detours, with their Knesset debates and their unyieldingly partisan, inflammatory rhetoric, do nothing to cool heated tempers or to foster prudent settlements. It is enough to imagine what would happen if the issue of yeshiva student exemptions needed to be hammered out in primary legislation to comprehend the potentially explosive, nonconsociational nature of such detours.

Fifth and last, court decisions, as noted earlier, are not attempts at mollifying the contending parties through finely balanced compromises and deals. On the contrary, court decisions are by their very character decisive resolutions to heated issues. Rarely do both sides emerge from a court ruling equally satisfied. When, for example, the courts are asked to evaluate the propriety of military exemptions for Haredim, the results of their deliberations will be dramatically different from a solution hammered out by political leaders of the religious and secular communities. This tendency to decisiveness renders the courts a problematic ally of the consociational style.

Still, it is important to add that judicial activism, in itself, does not necessarily subvert consociational arrangements. It can coexist with a politics of accommodation when its decisions are perceived by the contending parties as balanced and nonpartisan. In other words, consociational arrangements can persist when the court is understood to be above the fray, an ideologically undefined referee in the political contest. This would entail that its record of decisions straddle the religious-secular divide in a manner that could not be identified as belonging to one side or the other.

This, however, is clearly not the case; at very least, it is not how the religious community perceives the court. In their eyes, the court is a bulwark of liberal Western values in stark opposition to the normative Orthodox worldview. Its axioms are those of Western jurisprudence, and its views of human rights, gender equality, good government, the rights of minorities, and so on are those of Western jurists. Halacha has little if any influence on its decisions. Justice Barak minces no words in this regard. He writes that the definition of Israel as a Jewish and a democratic state does not involve a contradiction.

> The statement "Jewish and democratic" does not incorporate two opposites; rather it expresses accommodation and harmony. . . . We should understand this phrase at a level of abstraction so high that it will unify all members of this society and will seek what is common among them. The level of abstraction needs to be so high that it will agree with the democratic nature of the state. The state is indeed Jewish but not in the halachic-religious sense of the word. Therefore, we should not identify the values of the State of Israel as a Jewish state with those of Jewish law [mishpat ivry].[23]

The court is so thoroughly identified by the religious community with the liberal secular point of view that extremist threats on Justice Barak's life are not uncommon; these threats were taken so seriously by Israel's security services that he was assigned a full-time bodyguard. Even moderate religious figures like the late Zevulun Hammer, head of the National Religious Party, declared that "the religious and traditional communities feel themselves persecuted by government and the decisions of the Supreme Court."[24]

One of the most familiar rituals of nonconsociational politics in the last decade or so unfolds as follows: It begins with a savaging of the court and its members by some religious personage—notably, on this issue the differences between the national religious and Haredi parties is minimal. The court, it is charged, is a group of self-hating elitists, an unrepresentative coterie of secular Ashkenazi intellectuals, a privileged and inefficient group of heretics, and worse. (Rabbi Ovadiah Yosef, the spiritual leader of the Shas Party, spoke of the court's justices as ignoramuses who know less than even a six-year-old yeshiva student. He added that among their many other sins they "sleep with menstruating women [bo'alei nidot].") These attacks are followed by furious protests from the secularists, especially from the legal community. It is precisely these judges, they proclaim, that protect your rights, that ensure the rule of law, that save us all from the clutches of the "fundamentalist ayatollahs." If we listen closely to these vituperations, it becomes apparent that they are not directed toward particular issues. Notably, they speak in the context of the general struggle over the collective identity of the Jewish state, and it is just this that gives the debate its particularly venomous qualities.

One rather ordinary example will serve as an illustration. In the late spring of 1998, Yigal Bibi, the deputy minister of religion and a leading member of the National Religious Party, brashly rebuked the court in a Knesset speech. As to the court, he said sarcastically, "Everything is judicial activism, everything is lawless, everything is judiciable" and threatened that "if the Supreme Court persists in breaking the law, it will be necessary for us to make a law that [requires] the Supreme Court . . . to judge according to law." He ended with the assertion that "the time has come to say the emperor is naked."[25] (He may well have been responding to the comments that Justice Barak had made a week earlier: "He who claims that we should not adjudicate issues that have political consequences—doesn't know what law is all about.")[26] The secular response was fierce and predictable. In the end, Yigal Bibi was given a perfunctory slap on the wrist by some of his own NRP colleagues—although it is common knowledge that they agreed with the content if not the tone of his remarks. A meeting of reconciliation between an NRP leader and Justice Barak took place, and the issue was forgotten—for the time being.

The Supreme Court has played a significant part in undermining the consociational style. This is so in two regards: first, in regard to the controversial issues that it increasingly raises onto the public agenda, and second, in regard to the character of its judgments that—for the religious community, at least—make it an active partisan in the confrontation over the collective identity of the Jewish state.

The Constitutional Revolution and the Struggle over Collective Identity

In the second half of the 1980s, the struggle to enact a constitution for Israel was vigorously renewed. The driving force behind the effort was a group of academics who drafted a proposed constitution for Israel. They orchestrated a robust and many-sided campaign for its enactment, enlisting the support of key Knesset members and organizing mass public demonstrations.

Before discussing the practical consequences of this attempt at constitution drafting, it is of great interest to focus briefly on the phenomenon itself. Consociationalism is founded upon compromises and deals hammered out at the highest political levels. It requires well-defined communities controlled by forceful and broadly accepted political leaders. This leadership acts in the name of a constituency that is disciplined, perhaps even passive. Compacts between these leaders are negotiated far from public view and without the heated rhetoric of ideological confrontation. These agreements are then put into effect—from the top down.

Clearly, the presence of grassroots initiatives that mobilize support across communal lines, detour the normal political leadership, and bring the most sensitive issues into public view testifies to a weakening of the consociational style of politics. It speaks eloquently of the popular distrust of conventional political leadership, of the unwillingness to remain disciplined and passive, of deep dissatisfaction with the accommodationist style of the past, and of the readiness, indeed the burning desire, to cut through vexatious issues in a public, majoritarian way. The tens of thousands that gathered to support the movement known as A Constitution for Israel were there precisely because they refused to accept deals and compromises and because they wanted decisive action.[27]

In the early weeks and months of statehood, the drafting of a constitution was central to Israel's public agenda. Nevertheless, the effort never progressed beyond the stage of contentious discussion. Difficult issues of principle (the religious-secular divide) as well as political calculations (Ben-Gurion feared that a constitution would limit his political maneuvering room) frustrated the constitutional effort, which, in the end, produced a nebulous compromise: the Knesset, in the coming years, would pass a series of Basic Laws, which, when completed, would be "sewn" together into a constitutional document.

In practice, however, the Basic Laws enacted before the early 1990s were far from being constitutional in the familiar Western sense. Most of them had the status of ordinary legislation; they could be repealed easily enough by a plurality—even if it is not a majority of the members of the Knesset. Moreover, like ordinary laws, later legislation that contradicted its principles would nullify and supersede any of the Basic Laws. The principle, "A later law is superior to an earlier law," was valid for these Basic Laws, as well. Only a very few provisions were "entrenched" *(meshuryanim)*, that is, required an absolute majority of sixty-one members of the Knesset; but even this is, of course, a far cry from the arduous process of amending constitutions that is common in Western states. Lastly, the Basic Laws lacked any mention of fundamental human rights, a staple in all Western democratic constitutions.[28]

In 1992, as part of the general drive toward constitutionalism that A Constitution for Israel had inspired, the Knesset enacted two new Basic Laws: the Basic Law on Freedom of Occupation and the Basic Law on Human Freedom and Dignity. These Basic Laws are said to have produced a veritable constitutional revolution in Israel because they were categorically different from all previous Basic Laws. It should be said, for the sake of caution and balance, that there is a heated debate among jurists and judges as to whether this activist interpretation of the "revolution" is warranted. For our purposes we shall assume that the revolution has, in fact, taken place—for the simple reason that this is the position of Aharon Barak and other leading justices in today's Supreme Court. The two main proponents of a minimalist reading of the Basic Laws and of judicial restraint, Menachem Alon and Moshe Landau, have both retired from the bench.[29]

The process leading up to the legislation of the two new Basic Laws was tangled and complex; indeed, it contained all the major features of the religious-secular confrontation. It began with a relatively ambitious draft of the Basic Law on Human and Civil Rights, which passed a preliminary reading in the Knesset. It could progress no further, however, because of the dogged opposition of the religious parties and the decision of the larger secular parties to respect their wishes. In order to neutralize religious opposition, it was suggested that the ambitious and wide-ranging Basic Law on Human and Civil Rights be broken down into its component parts and that it be brought up for ratification part by part. In this way, at least those provisions to which the religious parties did not object could be passed.

In fact, it initially seemed clear enough that the Basic Law on Freedom of Occupation and the Basic Law on Human Freedom and Dignity were not objectionable on religious grounds. They did not, ostensibly, touch upon issues that had any religious bearing. By contrast, religiously sensitive provisions such as those protecting freedom of conscience and religion were omitted from the Basic Laws presented to the Knesset. Indeed, the two Basic Laws referred explicitly to the status quo arrangements and, in unambiguous language, authorized them. It stated that "nothing in this Basic Law should be understood as infringing the validity of laws that were valid before its enactment."[30]

Complementing all of this was the specific reference to Israel as a Jewish democracy. In the provisions elaborating the purpose of the Basic Laws, it was clearly asserted that they were intended to "anchor in the Basic Law the values of the State of Israel as a Jewish and democratic state." At first glance this seems like vintage consociationalism: each side received what was important to it, the secular focusing on the democratic nature of the state, the religious on its Jewish character.

However, the law confounded the intentions of the politicians, particularly the religious ones. From the moment of its passage, it led a life of its own, entirely out of the control of the hapless politicians who had conceived and voted for it. One jurist wrote at the time that both the religious and the secular camps took a calculated risk in passing the law; its practical consequences depended, in the event, on how the Supreme Court would interpret it.[31]

The constitutional revolution occasioned by these Basic Laws has two faces. First of all, human and civil rights previously based on precedents and on Israel's Declaration of Independence—the legal status of which were debatable and could be overcome by ordinary legislation—were now based upon unequivocal legislation enshrined in Basic Laws. Far more important, though, is the legal status the court attributed to its provisions. These Basic Laws, the court argued, are different from all the previous ones: they are more authoritative and more basic. Both of the Basic Laws, the court reasoned, contain a "restrictive clause" that specifically forbids infringing upon the rights guaranteed in the law. Only when this infringement "accords with the values of the State of Israel, is intended for a worthy purpose, and does not exceed what is necessary" is it acceptable. For the first time in Israel's legal history, the sovereignty of the Knesset had been explicitly limited. Henceforth, the court said in effect, all Knesset legislation must accord with the rights guaranteed by the two Basic Laws. If not, it would be judicially disqualified.[32]

Immediately following the passage of the two Basic Laws, a portentous political confrontation took place. In its wake, the Basic Law on Human Freedom and Dignity was altered, and the Basic Law on Freedom of Occupation was reformulated and passed once again. This confrontation and its consequences nicely illustrate how constitutional documents can undermine consociational accommodation. The typical progression here is as follows: It begins with the legislation of quasi-constitutional laws that undermine long-standing political arrangements. It continues with judicial activism, which now includes the monitoring of all legislation for its constitutionality. It ends with a spirited backlash in which the Haredi parties use all the numerical leverage at their command to change the law in ways that render it acceptable to Orthodox sensibilities.

The confrontation began with a dramatic court decision that based itself on the Basic Law on Freedom of Occupation. The Mitral Company was ordered by government officials to stop importing nonkosher meat. Mitral appealed to the court, which found in its favor. Importing meat, kosher or otherwise, was covered under the Basic Law on Freedom of Occupation. The court added that even a law specifically providing that nonkosher meat was not to be imported would be futile because freedom of occupation was covered by the restrictive clause in the Basic Law.[33] The religious parties objected vehemently. They were, among other things, stung by the realization that the Basic Law on Freedom of Occupation could have religious consequences. Indeed, they felt they had been duped into supporting the passage of a law that was now turned against them. For decades the accepted arrangement had been that the importation of meat required official approval, which was given in a selective and restricted way. The Supreme Court's decision undermined this customary practice and in so doing threatened to open a new and ominous front in the struggle over Jewish identity in Israel.

Shas, during this period, was the single religious party in the Labor-Rabin coalition. It sat in the government together with the aggressively secular party, Meretz—a fact that the other Haredi partners did not cease throwing up to the Shas leadership. Shas, to demonstrate its bona fides, felt compelled to precipitate a showdown over the Mitral decision. The status quo had been violated, they declared, and this was intolerable. For its part, the Labor Party was loathe to lose the single religious party in its coalition. The prospect that a peace government negotiating the Oslo agreement should rest its claim to legitimacy upon the extragovernmental support of the Arab parties was not at all appealing. Shas exploited its scale-tipping position with aplomb, and the constitutional revolution that had just been solemnly proclaimed was replaced by a constitutional counterrevolution. A new and highly convoluted provision was added to the Basic Law on Freedom of Occupation: "A law that infringes the freedom of occupation shall be valid even though it is not consistent with provision 4 [that is, even if the law is inconsistent with the restrictive clause] if included in the law that was passed by a majority of the members of the Knesset is an explicit provision stating that it is valid in spite of what is said in the Basic Law." A few moments after the passage of this revised Basic Law, the Knesset enacted the Importation of Meat Law (1994). One of its provisions, following the directive of the Basic Law passed a few moments earlier, read as follows: "This law is valid in spite of what is said in Basic Law: Freedom of Occupation."

It may well be that Israel is in the unique position of having a constitutional (or protoconstitutional) provision that can be detoured by ordinary legislation that simply declares itself valid despite what is said in the constitutional text. To be sure, the detouring law, it was stipulated, is valid only for a period of four years, but this, in practice, is not much of a limitation. Indeed, all it does is ensure that the charged religious-secular confrontation will repeat itself every four years, with all the deleterious consequences for consociational accommodation we have come to expect. To complete the chronology (at least up to the present moment), the law was renewed in March 1998 for a period of another four years—with all the rancor and malice that are appropriate to such confrontations.

From Meretz's point of view, the retreat from constitutional supremacy was a serious blow. To offset their losses, they demanded that the Basic Laws be emended as follows: the fundamental rights protected by these Basic Laws "will be honored in the spirit of the principles contained in Israel's Declaration of Independence." The wide-ranging principles mentioned in the Declaration of Independence include freedom of religion, nondiscrimination on the basis of origin, race, or religion, and a great deal more. Up to the passage of this amendment to the Basic Law, the court had ruled that the principles enshrined in the Declaration of Independence were only declaratory in character, that is, that they were not legally binding. Against the background of judicial activism and the Western liberal character of the court, however, it is entirely possible that the court will base itself on this new provision in order to justify a change in its position on the merely declaratory nature of the Declaration of Independence. This would surely set into motion another constitutional revolution, with all of its attendant anticonsociational repercussions.

Although the much-touted constitutional revolution has been weakened by detouring legislation, its effects are still being felt in the continuing struggle between consociationalism and majoritarian decisiveness. First of all, the Basic Laws protecting human and civil rights mean, in effect, that the courts have become the arbiters of what is and what is not a protected right. It is also quite possible that the courts, in the spirit of judicial activism, will interpret their mandate broadly and assertively.

Another sign of the times (which is inextricably related to the so-called constitutional revolution) is the continued pressure to finally draft and ratify an authoritative constitution for Israel. Despite the undoubted importance of the religious parties and their numerical indispensability for Netanyahu's government, the minister of justice (Tzachi Hanegbi) is, notably, persevering with plans to present the Knesset with a series of new Basic Laws on human and civil rights—including one related to freedom of religion. Even if these efforts are scuttled by religious pressures, they testify to an important change of atmosphere: a desire to establish publicly and legally what in the past would have been the subject of sub-rosa negotiations.

Second, there is the tendency of the court to understand its mandate in broad terms, even if the language of the law may appear quite specific and limited. To take a single example that has received attention in the juridical literature: although the principle of equality (in its various possible applications) is not clearly authorized in law, it would occasion little surprise were the court to interpret it broadly and forcefully.[34]

Third, despite the subversion of the constitutional revolution, an absolute majority is still necessary in order to revalidate the detouring legislation. The need to renew this legislation periodically promises the recurrence of public confrontations on incendiary religious issues. It cannot be doubted that ambitious politicians on both sides will exploit these debates, with their mobilizing potential, in order to find favor in the eyes of their constituents.

Fourth and last, however the specific struggles over these Basic Laws may play themselves out, it cannot be doubted that the very dispute over constitutional principles has become integral to the general confrontation over collective Jewish identity in the Jewish state. If the religious parties succeed in thwarting the drive toward a liberal, Western constitution, it will inflame the secular community. If, by contrast, the secularists prevail in passing a constitutional document informed by universal, liberal values, the religious community will be up in arms. In a word, constitutional pitched battles are precisely what consociational politics seeks to avoid.

How upsetting these Basic Laws are for the Haredi community can be gauged by a story currently making the political rounds. It is told that Aryeh Deri, the leader of the Shas Party, was made the following offer: support the legislation of the new Basic Laws and, in return, religious interests will be protected by law—even "entrenched" in a Basic Law specifically designed for this purpose. Deri answered with typical wit: I would not support even a Basic Law on the Ten Commandments, just because of the title, "Basic Law." Whether the story is real or apocryphal is beside the point; it accurately captures the traumatic effects of attempting to definitively articulate the collective identity and paramount values of the Jewish state.

In the course of the 1999 election campaign, the fraught confrontation between the religious communities and the courts (especially the Supreme Court) reached unprecedented heights. Whether the court and law enforcement systems ought to be regarded as rights-protecting heroes or as tradition-traducing villains became a central issue in the political contest. In 1998, a number of stress-laden judicial confrontations had accumulated—confrontations of principle that were perceived by the religious and especially by the Haredim as a broad-based assault on traditional religious values. Two of the most salient issues were the Supreme Court's decision that local religious councils needed to accept and include Conservative and Reform members in their ranks and—most confrontationist of all—its judgment that prevailing arrangements exempting yeshiva students from the draft could not stand as it was. The court remanded the question to the Knesset and gave it a year to legislate a reasonable resolution to this thorny issue.

In January 1999, a regional judge, Oded Aligon, expressed himself in a way that could be construed as characterizing the Haredim as "lice." David Yosef, the son of Ovadiah Yosef, responded by describing the judge as an anti-Semite.[35] These were merely the visible and public forms of discourse between the Haredi parties and the Israeli court system.

In February 1999, the religious leadership of the Haredi parties decided to hold a mass demonstration against the Supreme Court. Before the demonstration, the Supreme Court and especially its president, Aharon Barak, were denounced in exceptionally shrill and aggressive terms. Member of the Knesset Moshe Gafni from the Haredi Torah Judaism Party described Barak as "persecutor of the Jews" *(tzorer ha'Yehudim)*, a term normally reserved for Haman, the biblical enemy who had plotted to wipe out the Jewish people. Rabbi Ovadiah Yosef spoke of the courts' justices as "evil men *[resha'im]* because of whom all suffering is visited upon the world."[36] There was no dearth of calls for civil mutiny against the authorities. The demonstration's organizers spoke of their efforts as part of a war against the Supreme Court.[37] The intensity of this rhetoric prompted the law enforcement agencies to consider opening criminal investigations against a number of the more visible personalities involved, including Shas's leader, Rabbi Ovadiah Yosef, himself. The attorney general decided not to proceed with legal steps because he feared that a subpoena sent to a figure of Ovadiah Yosef's stature would be tantamount to a casus belli for the Haredi world. Predictably, an appeal to the Supreme Court followed the attorney general's demurral. The court was asked to override the attorney general's decision and to nevertheless place Ovadiah Yosef on trial.[38]

The demonstration against the Supreme Court took place in mid-February in Jerusalem, and it was one of the largest demonstrations in Israel's history. Estimations of the number of participants began at 250,000 and went up to nearly 400,000. A counterdemonstration, composed largely of secular Jews who wished to express solidarity with the Supreme Court, took place simultaneously, with about 50,000 participants. Thousands of police were deployed to preserve order because of the fear that the Haredim would march on the Supreme Court building. The dominant figure in the organization of the demonstration, the aged Rabbi Menachem Porush, long-time veteran of Haredi politics, emphasized that he was willing to "sacrifice his life against Justice Barak."[39]

It is important to return here to a theme we pursued earlier: the changing positions of the Haredi and national religious community. Whereas the National Religious Party (known then as Mizrahi) was the major protagonist for religious interests in the first generation after statehood (with the Haredim playing a subsidiary role), during the second generation—beginning especially in the early 1980s—the Haredi parties have taken on the mantle of leadership. This, as we have noted, exacerbates the conflict, for if the NRP constituency is Zionist and serves in the army, the Haredi parties are not and do not. This reversal of dominance and indecisiveness is clearly visible in the demonstration against the Supreme Court. In contrast with the clear and energetic Haredi decision to go forward with the demonstration, the national Zionist community was ambiguous and mealymouthed. Two of its main religious authorities, Rabbi Avraham Shapira and Rabbi Mordechai Eliyahu, supported and attended the demonstration, but its Knesset representatives spoke in dispirited tones and did not attend. The newspaper Ha'zofeh, the NRP's organ, opened its pages to a cacophony of opposed views; in the end the national religious community's position was hesitant, stammering, and indecisive.[40]

Before the demonstration's dust could settle, the next crisis loomed large: the verdict in the Aryeh Deri case. Deri had been convicted of serious crimes and sentenced to four years in prison, and the case became a central issue in the elections. It was charged by Deri and his supporters that the courts had been unfair to him, that he was an innocent martyr who only wished to serve his community but was, apparently, too successful for the tastes of the country's elites, and so on. Despite his conviction and sentencing (the court delayed his entrance to prison pending an appeal to the Supreme Court), Deri remained at the helm of the Shas Party. Moreover, Shas's entire campaign was focused on the person of Aryeh Deri and under the banner, "He's innocent." A very professional video cassette (showing the modesty in which Deri lived as opposed to the splendor of the judges' villas) was distributed by the tens of thousands. It carried Deri's impassioned arguments to the party faithful and doubtless swayed a considerable number of voters. The dramatic rise in Shas's Knesset representation—from ten to seventeen—cannot be dissociated from the antijudicial animus that drove their campaign.

Deri's trial was not perceived by the Shas faithful as the trial of a single individual. Shas's Eli Swissa, the minister of the interior, declared that "it was all of Shas that was on trial" and that Aryeh Deri was a sacrifice representing the entire movement with all its supporters and ideas.[41] There can be little doubt that Deri's trial, verdict, and sentence were crucial to the elections.

The Direct Election of the Prime Minister: Intentions and Effects

The drive to promulgate an authoritative charter for Israel resulted in the passage of yet another critical constitutional text, the Basic Law on the Government—popularly referred to as the Law for the Direct Election of the Prime Minister. It was passed in the spring of 1992 and put into practice for the first time in the elections of May 1996. (The law is complex and multifaceted; we touch upon only those elements that bear directly on our subject.) It is important to make a clear distinction between, on the one hand, the motives and intentions of its authors and, on the other, the practical consequences that ensued. These ostensibly unintended consequences have sparked a spirited attempt to nullify the law, an effort that passed a preliminary Knesset reading in the spring of 1998. Nevertheless, the future of this effort is quite uncertain because the leaders of the major parties, Benjamin Netanyahu and Ehud Barak, are among the law's most faithful supporters.

Originally, the law was intended to overcome the debilitating problems associated with a balanced two-camp system—to wit, the chronic instability of ruling coalitions, the "blackmail" potential in the hands of small but numerically indispensable parties, and the resulting inefficiency of government functioning. Until the late 1970s, the dominant-party system made for relative stability, clear leadership, and, in its own authoritarian and legally dubious ways, government efficiency. Because of Mapai dominance, the smaller parties were unable to exploit their bargaining position in exaggerated ways. Radical demands on the part of one party would only mean that Mapai would build its coalition with other more amenable partners. In a balanced two-camp system, by contrast, each party, small though it may be, can prove to be potentially pivotal in forming a coalition. Indeed, at times, the life of the government rested upon the support of a single member of the Knesset who was able to name his price and get it. The intensity of public dissatisfaction with this state of affairs went from fervent to feverish, but it required a truly scandalous government crisis to convert this malaise into practical legislation.

The government crisis in the spring of 1990, popularly spoken of as the *targil masri'ach* (the stinking scheme), provided necessary and sufficient cause to justify a radical constitutional revision. The crisis lasted for four months and dramatically highlighted the egregious ills of the system. For the first time in Israel's parliamentary history a government fell on a no-confidence vote, which was part of an elaborate scheme concocted by Shimon Peres to create a Labor government in place of the National Unity government of Labor and Likud that had been in power since 1988.

But the plan backfired. Single members of the Knesset, often individuals with whom the public had little or no familiarity, pedaled their wares between the large parties and unashamedly sold them to the highest bidder. One day it looked as if Labor had the numbers to establish a government; on the next, it appeared that the pendulum had swung in the Likud's favor. The cynicism and corruption reached unprecedented heights when some long-time Knesset members switched party affiliations, leaving one party and joining the other with the explicit promise of ministerial posts, budgets, et cetera. After a roller-coaster experience of blackmail, promises, threats, and humiliations, the crisis ended with the formation of a Likud government. It was also the direct catalyst for the Basic Law on the Government.[42]

At the heart of the Basic Law is the (quasi-presidential) direct election of the prime minister. Direct election eliminates the possibility—so painfully evident in the targil masri'ach—that small parties, even isolated individuals, will control the future of the country. Its avowed purpose is to radically transform the nature of coalitional negotiations following the election: The victor in the prime ministerial elections is, by dint of popular support, the prime minister. It is he or she, and he or she alone, who will form the coalition; there is no negotiating this central point. In the old system, the two major parties competed for the smaller party's allegiance, without which they could not create a viable government. Direct election is meant to reverse this relationship. Henceforth, the smaller parties will compete among themselves to determine which one will be chosen by the elected prime minister to join in the government he or she will form. Under these circumstances the small parties' political leverage is substantially diminished.

The new system attempts to substantially augment the power of the prime minister.[43] Owing to the mandate received in majoritarian elections, the prime minister now wields decisive power vis-à-vis his coalitional partners. Direct election aims to cut through the tangle of small-party demands—especially those of Haredi parties—in other words, to restore power to the majority, embodied in the person of the prime minister. The law's authors were interested in investing the prime minister with the kind of conclusive power that would obviate the need for nerve-racking give-and-take, for compromises and arrangements, for accommodating the demands of the religious minority. The great public support for direct election in the early 1990s reflected a growing impatience with consociational concessions—concessions that were more and more seen as coalitional extortion rather than large-party largesse.

Direct election means taking power away from the various political elites and investing it in the public at large. This is tantamount to dismantling the central plank of the consociational program. No longer do political leaders representing the various communities negotiate arrangements with one another far from the public eye. Electoral victory resolves the issues sharply and definitively. Indeed, part of the current opposition to direct election resides in the fear that it tends to encourage an irresponsible populist style in Israeli politics.

Not only does direct election seek to weaken the negotiating position of the smaller parties, it also makes it far more dangerous for small parties in the coalition to challenge the policies of a sitting prime minister.

Under the old system, the threat of leaving the coalition was a powerful incentive used regularly by the smaller parties to "discipline" a recalcitrant prime minister. In effect, the smaller parties could compel the prime minister to negotiate with them while the sword of Damocles hung threateningly above the coalition's integrity. The new Basic Law seeks to eliminate this possibility and in so doing to shore up the coalition's stability. Not only does the law require sixty-one members of the Knesset to vote no confidence (as opposed to a simple plurality in the past), it now stipulates that a vote of no confidence is a vote to dissolve the Knesset and to hold new elections for both the post of prime minister and the Knesset. The prospect of losing one's parliamentary seat is a powerful incentive that makes coalition partners far more wary of challenging the prime minister.

Beyond its express political purposes, the electoral reality created by direct election also deals a sharp blow to consociationalist accommodation. In the old system, under which the vote was limited to choosing a single party, the resulting electoral map was complex and multidimensional—divided as it was between ten to fifteen parties of very diverse character. Although these parties could be defined ideologically, there was no overwhelming sense of one large ideological community facing off against the other. Differences were mediated and deflected by party distinctiveness, by the subdivisions and rivalries that made the electoral map so dauntingly intricate. To be sure, there were large camps of like-minded parties, but the electoral system did not force a victory by majority, so the line of demarcation between the two was blurred and equivocal.

Direct election, by contrast, underscores—indeed, it bodies forth—the two-camp reality that dominates Israeli politics. The sense of "us and them" has never been so explicit and unmistakable as in the electoral campaign of 1996. The deep cleavages that were occluded under the old system are dramatically exposed and emphasized in the new one. Moreover, the demographic lines of demarcation between the two communities have become common knowledge, indeed, often identifiable by the naked eye—so much so, in fact, that in an unprecedented way the Likud and the religious parties helped each other in getting out the vote while Labor and Meretz similarly pooled their resources. More than 90 percent of the religious community voted for Netanyahu, whereas the lion's share of secularists voted for Peres.[44] Sephardi and Ashkenazi origins, educational attainments, and economic status were also highly significant in dividing the vote between the two communities. A coalition of the "marginals"—the religious, Haredim, Sephardim, and new immigrants—overcame a coalition of mainstream "Israelis" associated with Labor and Meretz.[45] Clearly, it is this kind of manifest confrontation between two clearly defined communities over matters of high principle that is consociationalism's anathema. The prospects of accommodation become hopeless and irrelevant when communities struggle with one another explicitly and publicly at the level of ideological principle, when negotiations between different communal elites is replaced by a direct and popular vote.

One pointed expression of this heightened sense of confrontation, of winners and losers, of "us and them," is the energy that Ehud Barak, the leader of the Labor Party, has invested in the issue of military service for yeshiva students. Although the displeasure of the great majority of Israelis with the Haredi exemption from military service is hardly new, only in 1998 has the issue become a central plank in Barak's political program. Previously it was seen as an unfortunate but probably necessary component of the status quo arrangement.

In the face of profound Haredi opposition, Barak initiated a public campaign under the slogan, "One people, one draft" (*Am echad, giyus echad*). (Notably, this slogan is a provocative take-off on another slogan supported by the religious community, "One people, one conversion" [*Am echad, giyur echad*].) Barak appealed explicitly to the vast majority of Israelis for whom the Haredi exemption is unconscionable. He called for the majority to exercise its sovereignty decisively. (There is little doubt that this issue was taken up by the Labor Party leadership in the wake of public opinion surveys that revealed the depth of mass opposition to the arrangement.)

If only briefly and in closing, it should be mentioned that the candidacy of Tel Aviv's mayor, Roni Milo, for the prime ministerial post is openly based upon the great surge of current anti-Haredi public opinion. In his announcement he made it clear that he would not be seeking Haredi support—an unprecedented act in Israeli public life. As explicitly as he could, Milo founded his campaign on the insufferable power of the Haredi parties. Like Barak, he overcame traditional consociational cautions and set himself on a collision course with the Haredi community. The immanent majoritarian and anticonsociational logic of direct election could not have been more lucidly expressed.

Chapter Five

Demographic, Cultural, and Religious Changes

Consociationalism under Pressure

The struggle over Jewish identity is fought on many fronts. Distinguishing among them and presenting them as distinct phenomena, although necessary for the sake of clarity, violates the sense of a seamless reality in which one issue shades off into another and one concern is the complement and counterpart of another. We have already taken up historical, political, party-related, and constitutional subjects; but these are inextricably related to the major social, demographic, religious, and cultural transformations that have profoundly altered the way Israelis live. This chapter is devoted to an exploration of these factors. What unifies all of them, we claim, is the way in which they create a public sphere that is fundamentally inhospitable to consociational accommodation.

The Media and the Decline of Consociational Democracy

The term *revolution* is entirely appropriate to describe the way Israel's electronic media have changed in the 1990s. First of all, the sheer quantity of viewing and listening options has made a geometric leap forward. A country with a single government-sponsored TV channel in the 1980s, Israel today offers cable subscribers (about 65 percent of Israeli households) with roughly forty viewing channels, including many from the United States, Britain, France, Germany, and Russia. A second Israeli TV channel has been added, and there is talk of yet a third in the future. There has been a parallel explosion in radio channels. Some of them, to be sure, are "pirate" stations, but they have been broadcasting without serious government intervention for years. Moreover, as opposed to the past, when broadcasting was a government monopoly, today most of the new TV and radio stations are controlled by private interests. In a word, they now operate as commercial businesses.[1] The change is significant not only in scale but also in time: it was condensed into a short span of seven or eight years—as opposed to the decades in which these processes normally unfold in the Western world.

As is well known, the media present the news, but they also frame, organize, and interpret it. In large measure, the media shape the political agenda. It should be clear to the reader that our study relies heavily on the news as presented by the media (especially the written press) as a prime source for current developments in religious-secular relations. When changes are rapid, far-ranging, and current, relying on the daily press is quite inevitable. It is not, however, the media's factual presentation of the news to which we devote this section. We are here interested in exploring the role of the media as the fashioners and creators of the news, indeed, as another powerful player in the religious-secular struggle.

Not so long ago, Israel's daily newspapers were mostly political in character, that is, they were the organs of clearly defined parties and political communities—left, right, religious, Haredi, and so on. For the most part (except for the religious and Haredi organs) this kind of "mobilized" newspaper has disappeared. In its place, commercial newspapers now dominate the market. This transformation was accompanied by a change in the character of newspaper journalism. In contrast with a media that served to forward the basic Zionist aims of rebuilding the land and the ingathering of the Exile, today's newspapers are far closer in character to those published in Western democracies. Aggressive investigatory reporting that seeks to reveal the scandal behind the scenes has become common. Because "good news" is often no news at all, the papers tend to focus on the problematic, the exceptional, the eye-catching headline. As such, the media have become an active part in the religious-secular conflict.

Consociationalism, we have noted, often rests on "deals" made between leaders of the various communities. Often these deals—although they lubricate the wheels of politics—are not strictly in accordance with the high standards of "good government" (mimshal takin). Political appointments and payoffs often take precedence over merit or worthiness. In the past, these deals were largely occluded and unreported. Today, an army of reporters eager to make a career are on the trail of any such telltale misbehavior. As we emphasize in the following section, this un-precedented vigilance, the kind of fishbowl politics that aggressively tracks down backroom deals, renders many of the consociational ar-rangements too public and transparent to be workable.

Beyond its aggressively investigatory character, however, the media are often not disposed to present controversial issues in a fair-minded, balanced, and complex way. As one reporter (who will remain anony-mous) opined: If you want balance and complexity, go to the academic literature; newspapers need to sell, and complexity does not sell. A few examples will suffice. In 1998, *Ha'aretz*, Israel's prestige newspaper, ran a series of reports on Haredi life.[2] As the Haredi community becomes more and more pivotal politically, it is only natural that the coverage of their lives and doings grow apace. At one level it was simple descriptive reportage that depicted a reality the paper's (mostly secular and West-ern) readership was interested to learn more about.

Yet the picture that emerged from the report was not so much inac-curate as the kind of one-sided, revelatory presentation that is so com-mon in investigatory journalism. It emphasized those elements of Haredi life that made for good newspaper copy and occluded those that made for a more complicated picture. As it emerged from the series, there was little or nothing positive about Haredi life, no beauty in their faith, nor in their learning, nor in their communal solidarity, nor in their charita-ble activities. The Haredi world was portrayed as predatory, parasitical, corrupt, and almost uniformly repellent.[3] It should be said, for the sake of balance, that the image of secular Israel that appears in the Haredi press is at least equally hostile and misleading. These lopsided images are not merely roughly accurate reflections of what the religious and sec-ular communities think of each other; they are also catalysts that reen-force, indeed radicalize, both communities.

When presented without balance and out of context, much of the world of Halacha appears exotic, even preposterous, in secular eyes—and the converse is also true. There is, of course, a fundamental clash of cultures and worldviews between Halacha and liberal Western percep-tions, and it is only to be expected that they will appear odd in each oth-ers' eyes. Yet when the Haredi newspapers present the world of secular Israeli youth as mindless, immoral, drugged, and unspeakably lewd, this becomes an active part of the religious-secular conflict, not merely a reflection of it.

Similarly, when the secular press cites halachic decisions that have no implications for public life, out of context and for their sensational or comic value, the conflict is not merely expressed, it is exacerbated. Those halachic decisions that are reasonable and wise are not considered newsworthy; but those that are laughable and grotesque (at least, from a secular viewpoint) become grist for the culture war's mill—presented as yet further proof that the other side is hopelessly Neanderthal and not to be taken seriously. A striking example relates to Rabbi Ovadiah Yosef's declaration that picking one's nose on the Sabbath is prohibited. The publication of the prohibition *tout court,* out of context, without the entire learned and complex discussion of Sabbath observance in which it was embedded, rendered it simply ludicrous. The point of the publication was, in fact, to make the other side a laughing stock. Not surprisingly, virtually all the satirical TV programs and caricaturists could not resist the temptation. One devastating burlesque suggested that the Druze (acting in the age-old role of *Shabbos goyim)* could act as nose pickers for the Jews on the Sabbath. (This was also a clear reference to the fact that Druze inspectors are employed by the Ministry of Labor to fine shops open on the Sabbath.) Notably, when Rabbi Yosef declares that "saving lives is preferable to keeping the territories"—a courageous decision of incomparably greater moral character and practical importance, one applauded by the Israeli left—it is given relatively short shrift by the media.[4]

The Haredi press, for its part, is every bit as belligerent and dismissive—and then some. Apart from the recurrent images of drug-crazed, sybaritic, terminally empty-headed young people, the secular world is also portrayed as spitefully anti-Semitic. Only self-hate can explain their revolt against Halacha and traditional Jewish values. At times, secular Jews are even compared with Nazis. One example was a call to "plow over the kibbuzim" *(lacharosh et hakibutzim)* and to bring them to trial in a "Nuremberg-like court" *(bevet din nusach Nuremberg).*[5] So outlandish have these Haredi attacks become that Israel's attorney general has intervened to warn various Haredi editors and publishers that they have passed the "red line" between expressing a point of view and indulging in libelous provocations.[6]

Massive media presence also undermines the protagonists' ability to work out viable compromises. (This is meant not as a critique of the media but rather as a description of the dynamics of a media-centered society.) Recall the drama surrounding the drafting of Israel's Declara-

tion of Independence and the difficulties over the inclusion or noninclu-
sion of reference to "the God of Israel": what if this founding moment
of the State of Israel had received the kind of first-hand treatment common in the contemporary media? It takes little imagination to conclude
that the issues would have been enthusiastically joined by all and sundry,
high-principled declarations would have been heard, and impassible ideological barricades would have been erected on all sides. In a word, the
Declaration of Independence would not have been signed.

The media publicizes issues, makes them the talk of the town (otherwise known as the public agenda), and, hence, prevents them from being
dealt with in discreet and practical ways. This is certainly the case in regard to the most divisive issue in recent memory: the controversy over the
central performance marking fifty years of Israeli statehood—Pa'amonei
Yovel (Jubilee Bells). Israel's premier ballet troupe (Bat Sheva) was to
perform a dance (which they had often performed in concert) to a traditional Jewish text and melody ("Echad Mee Yoday'ah"). The ballet
involved the dancers' stripping off of their outer clothing and being left
in long johns—and less. When the Haredi leaders learned of this they
responded, in effect, "Over our dead bodies." The ballet troupe, for its
part, regarded the issue as a quintessential case of artistic freedom and
freedom of speech. Quite soon, however, it was being presented as a principled clash between enlightened Western civilization, on the one side,
and primitive religious obscurantism, on the other. Religious spokespersons denounced the ballet troupe for what they saw as a deliberate
attempt at blasphemy, a ridiculing of a holy text justified only because
the dancers were so-called artists, licensed to do what they pleased whatever the offense to others.

Because of the media hype surrounding this incident, the conflict was
unresolvable. It had become too much of a principled public issue—an
issue in which the radicals rather than the moderates set the tone. Compromise solutions (such as performing the dance in more modest clothing) were angrily rejected. It was hard for either side to back down when
the issues were seen as principled and essential. As performance time
drew near, the media aired increasingly do-or-die statements from all
sides. In the end, the troupe refused to perform and left the theater.

This intense public collision left a deep scar on the Israeli polity—one
with repercussions beyond the Pa'amonei Yovel performance. It was,
notably, a controversy over the shape and nature of Jewish public space
and identity, that is, the collective character of Jewish Israel. The aggres-

sive media presence, with its inherent tendency to transform practical problems into questions of ideology, creed, and dogma, was, in some significant sense, responsible for the inability to find a pragmatic modus vivendi (like the one that was found for the Declaration of Independence).

The media subvert another of the essential qualities of consociational politics: the autonomy and separateness of the participating communities. When the communities are separate and discrete, their respective political leaderships can hammer out consociational arrangements. Although the Haredi population are overwhelmingly concentrated in Haredi towns and neighborhoods, the contemporary media tend to blur the kind of separateness that was possible only a generation ago. Although it is difficult to gauge the exact degree to which radio, TV, and the secular press enter into Haredi homes—they are publicly frowned upon—there is little doubt that substantial inroads are made. The exposure to secular life and values is probably more extensive than what the Haredi world would like to admit. The communities are not quite as hermetically sealed off from each other as in the past.

Perhaps even more important, the Haredi portrayal of secular society as dissolute and self-hating is an old theme pursued even before 1948. The proliferation of media channels and investigatory reporting in the 1980s and 1990s, however, has catapulted these previously in-house, community-bounded publications into the public domain. Each of the major secular newspapers has a team checking the weekly harvest from the Haredi press, and, of course, it is only the more perverse and incendiary comments that are reported in the secular press. No surprise, then, that secular attitudes toward the Haredi world grow surly and intolerant.

The Decline of "Illegalism" and the Growing Insistence on Good Government

In a broad and insightful analysis, Ehud Sprintzak contends that "illegalism" is one of the most basic and long-standing characteristics of Israeli political culture.[7] Illegalism is defined as a tendency to view the legal system, indeed, the rule of law itself, in instrumental terms. Obedience derives not from the intrinsic, principled validity of law but rather from its utility in serving other more basic interests. Illegalism has been associated with the densely familial quality of Israeli social life. This informal, ascriptive, and personalized approach to public life overrides and undermines the formal, self-standing qualities that we normally associate with the rule of law.

Although contemporary Israel is generally regarded as a liberal democratic state (with some well-known deviations and exceptions), liberal democracy has a rather tenuous and not very lengthy presence in Zionist history. During the Yishuv era, the three major ideological blocs had only a passing relationship with the liberal tradition. The socialists (both radical and moderate) were closer to the spirit of Karl Marx than that of John Stuart Mill. Moreover, the term *burgani* (bourgeois) was considered a deadly insult. The rule of law and the idea of good government were less meaningful to them than the success of the socialist-Zionist vision as they saw it. Ben-Gurion, their most prominent leader, was notorious for his rather cavalier attitude toward democratic and liberal principles.

Neither did the right wing, as represented by the Herut Party, have a deep commitment to liberal democratic principles. Democracy was not their ideological goal. It was the nation (like socialism for the left) that demanded absolute obedience. Indeed, liberal democracy, in their view, was often associated with decadence, spiritlessness, and impotence. At times, the right wing overtly flirted with fascism.

The religious community as represented by the Mizrahi related to democracy in an instrumental way, as well. Halacha certainly did not prescribe liberal democracy. At best, democracy was a practical means by which to relate to the other political forces within the Yishuv. Liberal principles such as good government, individual rights, and the rule of law made only superficial inroads in the religious community.

The founding of the state did not substantially change this instrumental approach to democracy. Principled commitment to democratic ideals and individual rights remained rather shallow and erratic. All agreed that democracy was necessary because it was the only context fair enough to induce the various political protagonists to engage one another in the public sphere. All sides knew that without the precepts of fair play and majority rule, the young polity was in danger of coming apart. There were those for whom democratic forms recommended themselves for more cynical reasons, as well: they would allow elegant manipulation, even exploitation, of other groups.

Only rather late in Israel's political history do authentically liberal ideas permeate the public sphere. It is difficult to date such nebulous changes in consciousness, but liberalism seems to have picked up its initial momentum during the early 1970s. The aftermath of the Yom Kippur war, in which an enraged public insisted that those responsible be sacked, may be taken as a beginning (if a somewhat arbitrary one). The Likud's rise to power in 1977 may be another. Nevertheless, if its origins are difficult to specify, the same cannot be said of the complex of causes that underlay it. The erosion of systematic ideologies (both left and right) created a vacuum into which liberal ideas could easily enter. Needless to say, the more recent collapse of communism and emergence of the "global village" contributed their share. Israel was no longer an isolated and remote state that developed along its own trajectory; it was now fully a part of the liberal Western world. The massive influence of American culture certainly carried American political ideas with it. The values of the United States, both as the most powerful nation in the world and as Israel's main political ally, percolated into Israeli culture in a sweeping way. Moreover, hundreds of thousands of Israelis traveled to the United States and Western Europe—often as representatives of Israeli organizations, that is, for long periods of time—and became aware of different standards of public accountability. Overwhelmingly, Israeli academics did their graduate studies in the United States and Western Europe. Upon their return to Israel, they became powerful emissaries of Western political ideas. The media revolution, as well as the internet, brought American and Western ideas to Israelis as never before.

With the decline of both socialist Zionism and the dirigiste style of politics, Israel has more and more come to adopt the liberal ideal of good government. The older form of ascriptive, informal, illegalist politics was discredited just as the demand for accountability, popular control, and bureaucratic rationality grew apace. Signs of this transformation are readily visible: the laws mandating intraparty democracy and financial accountability, the substitution of open party primaries for dubious appointment committees (despite certain recent regressions), the necessity to publish all deals made between parties prior to the elections, the growing resistance to blatant political appointments, to name but a few.

Another striking instance of this process is the growing prestige and influence of the state comptroller. In the past, the yearly comptroller reports detailing questionable and even criminal activity in government were shelved almost as quickly as they appeared. The public sense that lamentable practices such as these were an inevitable part of the functioning of government led to cynicism and resignation. Relying on the current demand for good government, the state comptroller has become more aggressive and considerably more effective, and the public outcry against questionable practices has become considerably more difficult to silence. Comptroller reports have ended in important indictments and major changes in bureaucratic procedure. They have led, among other things, to a number of celebrated trials in which members of the Knesset and government ministers have been accused of malfeasance and, in some cases, even jailed. Interestingly, their argument that these were standard practices in the past have fallen on deaf ears.

Moreover, a spate of public organizations whose purpose it is to advance the cause of good government and to monitor governmental practices has become quite important in recent years. Most of these organizations are new, having been established at the end of the 1980s and especially in the early 1990s. (The major catalyst was the shockingly unscrupulous coalitional negotiations of those years.) Starting with groups that support the effort to draft a constitution and continuing to others that deal specifically with human rights violations and religious coercion and those that observe and assess government performance in terms of accountability, legality, and efficiency, these watchdog groups have more and more become a familiar fixture in Israeli public life. They regularly blow the whistle on improprieties and ethical shortcuts in governmental activity—indeed, they often appeal to the courts for redress. A very partial list would include the Movement for Good Government (Ha'tnua le'aychut ha'shilton), A Constitution for Israel, Chemdat, Achi, Amitai, Am Chofshee, Betzelem, the League for Civil Rights in Israel, and the Focus for Protecting the Individual. (Notably, a preliminary study revealed that more than a third of the appeals to the Supreme Court of the Movement for Good Government—perhaps the most central of the "good government" organizations—were related to religious issues.) All this clearly renders covert accommodationist deals more problematic to reach and more difficult to abide by. (Many of these organizations, it is interesting to note, rely on the tendency of the current judicially activist court to grant legal standing to groups that lack a direct stake in particular legislation.)

We have repeatedly emphasized that consociationalism rests on discreet, informal understandings between political elites. Their ability to come to tactical agreements and tension-relieving compromises—often far from the public eye—prevents the issues in contention from becoming principled and public, in which case they would be far more difficult to resolve. This, as we have noted, is one of the most fundamental sources of Orthodox hegemony and autonomy. It is perhaps nowhere more strikingly present than in the budgeting for religious institutions, especially those of the Haredim. Budgeting for them often does not follow the normal rules of good government, such as the indiscriminate application of systemwide criteria to all institutions requesting funding. Haredi religious institutions are substantially supported by the so-called special funds *(k'safim yichudi'im)* allotted according to political and coalitional clout rather than on the basis of merit.

Consociationalism is, of course, not necessarily linked with illegalism. In Israel, however, the connection is manifest. Special funding and political appointments in the illegalist style are among the most important means by which the coalition maker repays its partners for their services. Notably, when coalitional negotiations took place in the 1980s, Agudat Israel demanded and received the chair of the Knesset's powerful financial committee to insure that its funding would continue unabated. For decades there were all manner of quotas and party keys for the allotment of public-sector jobs that sidestepped criteria of merit and often paid only scant attention to the candidates' personal credentials. In effect, illegalism was a critical lubricant for consociationalism's wheels. It provided political elites with the necessary latitude to broker truce-sustaining deals in matters of religion and state.

Sprintzak speculates that the "legalization" of Israeli public life might take place if a constitution were adopted and if public pressure were to become intense. Notably, both of these conditions seem to be in the process of emerging. We have already discussed the protoconstitutional Basic Laws that were adopted in the early 1990s. At least as important is the growing insistence on good government and the concomitant public rejection of the proverbial smoke-filled room with its shady deals.

Sensing the breakdown of the older consociational patterns, the religious parties have reacted with anger and dismay. They were especially offended by the actions of the previous minister of religion (Shimon Shitrit, who was non-Orthodox and from the Labor Party), who announced his intention to apply the criteria of transparency, public welfare, and bureaucratic rationality to all those groups funded by his ministry. When a group of rabbinic leaders vehemently protested this policy—to the point of verbally declaring war on the government—the minister's office responded that these pressures would not deter him from his resolve to institute the rules of good government to the field of religious services. Notably, the opposition of the ultra-Orthodox United Torah Judaism Party to the Oslo B Agreement was not couched in terms of its hawkish views or even in terms of the indivisibility of the biblical homeland; rather, it refused to vote for anything supported by a government that has thrown out the *talit* (prayer shawl) and *tephilin* (phylacteries). It was even proposed (though never implemented) that the religious parties abstain on the Oslo B Agreement vote in return for the removal of the minister of religion.

Non-Jews in a Jewish Society: Jewish Identity and the Immigration from the Former Soviet Union

The rapid dissolution of the Soviet Union at the end of the 1980s set off a monumental wave of immigration to Israel. Nothing like it had happened since the early 1950s. In the relatively short space of a decade, Israel absorbed roughly eight hundred thousand new immigrants—increasing its population from five million to six million. The rate of immigration was especially high in the early 1990s, when some six hundred thousand immigrants arrived. In the late 1990s the immigration rate has slowed substantially, but still, even in this period, it continues to be significant. It was obvious to all that this wave of immigration would profoundly affect the demographic composition of Israel. Quantitatively, the immigrants constituted 13 percent of Israel's total population and 15 percent of its Jewish population. Former Soviet citizens became the largest group of origin (passing those of Moroccan extraction) in Israeli society.[8] In two complementary ways this wave of immigrants is of cardinal importance for our purposes: first of all, their overwhelmingly secular character, and second, the large percentage among them who are halachically non-Jews.

In an in-depth study of the 1992 elections, one observer has concluded that the Soviet immigrants behave much like veteran Israelis in most areas except one: their religious (more accurately, nonreligious) tendencies—they are overwhelmingly secular in outlook and practice. The study speculates that this is one of the sources of their vote for the Labor Party in the 1992 elections. Because the Likud was more identified with religious parties, these immigrants voted for its major competitor.[9] Another student of these new immigrants reports that some 90 percent among them support civil marriage, public transport on the Sabbath, and other liberal and secular practices. He emphasizes that "if these opinions will be recruited for political purposes . . . they will likely change the basic patterns of life in Israel."[10] A well-placed Russian-language journalist argues that most immigrants feel distance and alienation from the religious practices and conventions as they have been institutionalized in Israel. Like other secular protagonists, she calls for freedom of religion, most especially in regard to the new immigrants.[11]

The Sephardic Chief Rabbi Bakshi-Doron has expressed his concerns about the nonreligious character of this new wave of immigration. He fears they will play a leading role in the secularization of Israeli society. He has called attention to the unprecedented number of stores that sell pork—their number, according to various estimates, runs to about six hundred—and contends that the overwhelming majority of Israelis in the past did not eat pork, which was deemed improper in broadly national rather than specifically religious terms. Pork, as opposed to other non-kosher foods, has a particularly stinging and charged quality about it. It is the archetypical symbol of Jewish difference. The Chief Rabbi pessimistically concludes that "religious laws will collapse and religion will be separated from the state" if vigorous countermeasures are not taken.[12]

In the 1990s there were a number of confrontations over stores' selling pork. In a few cases, proprietors appealed to the courts, claiming that their stores were protected against municipal statutes by the Freedom of Occupation law. Part of the problem no doubt arose because the immigrants were often settled in "development" towns, whose populations tend to be largely traditional and religious—particularly so in regard to the offensive consumption of pork. In any event, many of these stores continue to operate—whatever the municipal statutes may say.[13]

We have noted (in chapter 2) that despite the energetic attempts of the minister of labor to close shopping centers on the Sabbath in accordance with the law, his efforts could not resist the basic changes in consumption, shopping, and leisure patterns that have transformed Israeli society. The power of large-scale demographic transformations and broad-based social trends is greater than that of any law or statute. Appealing to a law that overtly violates the prevalent patterns of behavior will only make this law one more point of contention in the confrontation between religious and secular Israelis.

It might be argued that this special nonreligious character of immigrants from the former Soviet Union is merely a temporary phenomenon that will fade as they become more integrated into Israeli society. In truth, however, this is highly unlikely: First, these immigrants tend to preserve their linguistic and cultural uniqueness. One informed observer of the new immigrants' reality reports that by comparison with the Soviet immigration of the 1970s that "marched enthusiastically toward the 'melting pot,'" the recent immigrants move "instinctively toward the preservation of their linguistic and cultural uniqueness." Moreover, with the decline of the melting-pot ideology, preserving their own cultural uniqueness is far more acceptable today than it ever was in the past.[14]

Second, the secular character of the immigrants is not an attribute that is new to Israeli society. It is not as if they were introducing foreign norms into a resisting collective. A large secular community already exists, and the "Russian" community merely blends into a prevailing trait of Israeli society. In fact, militant secularists often declare their determination to recruit the new immigrants to their position. For example, Yossi Sarid, the leader of the Meretz Party, writes a regular column in *Vesty,* one of the larger newspapers in the Russian language. As a general rule, the secular militants among veteran Israelis seem more radical in their secularity than the Russians; indeed, their goal appears to be the radicalization of the immigrant community.[15]

Finally, many of the immigrants are not, halachically speaking, Jews. They are nonetheless closely related—familially and communally—to many who are. Under such circumstances it is unlikely that they will be sympathetic to the Orthodox establishment that seeks to place all manner of obstacles and disqualifications in the path of their non-Jewish spouses, children, or friends. Among the many religious-secular concerns raised by the recent wave of immigration, the issue of non-Jews (by halachic definitions) in the Israeli collective is the most pressing and essential. It tends to subvert the very possibility of consociational accommodation.

Until 1970, the Law of Return declared that all Jews have a right to return to the homeland. Nowhere, however, did the law define clearly who is a Jew or what criteria would be used in making such a determination. The amendment to the Law of Return passed in that year combines two elements that, taken together, provide an excellent summary of the dilemma facing the halachically non-Jewish immigrants. On the one hand, the law states that a Jew is someone "born to a Jewish mother, and is not a member of another faith, or someone who has converted." This rather rigorously formulated provision reflects the demands of the religious parties. On the other hand, however, the law provides that the right to immigrate to Israel and to receive Israeli citizenship will be sweepingly offered to "a child or grandchild of a Jew, to the spouse of a Jew, and to the spouse of a child or grandchild of a Jew." What is more, the law provides that these rights will be given even in cases where the Jew chooses not to immigrate or is no longer alive.

How did such a law come to be? An even more curious question, why did the religious parties allow it to pass? Paradoxically, it was just the rigorous language defining who is a Jew that necessitated the loose formulation regarding the question of who can be considered an oleh. Fearing that intermarried potential immigrants would not come to Israel because their spouses, children, and grandchildren could not join them, the law construes the right to *aliya* (citizenship) very liberally. When the law was drafted, it was thought to be a way of allowing a few mixed families to immigrate. As Uri Gordon, head of the aliya section in the Jewish Agency, put it, the emendation to the law, "which was meant to deal with a few exceptional cases, was transformed over time to an automatic entrance ticket to many non-Jews, out of all proportion to what is reasonable." [16]

It is difficult to accurately estimate the number of non-Jews among the immigrants. The lowest numbers speak of 10 percent, the highest of 40 percent. One researcher who studied the Jewishness of the immigrants in 1993 argues that the later the immigration date, the larger the percentage of couples in which one of the partners is a non-Jew. [17] This tendency has apparently grown more and more salient in recent years. In the second half of the 1990s published reports claim that a majority of those arriving are not Jews. [18] Even if we accept the lower estimates, it is clear that this represents a novel and formidable challenge to Israeli society generally and to the texture of religious-secular relations more specifically. For the first time, Israel will need to deal with a large number of non-Jews who are not Arabs and who wish to integrate into Jewish Israel.

The "Who is a Jew?" question is, of course, not new to Israeli society. The dramatic novelty in this case is that "Who is a Jew?" ceases to be a question of principle that affects only a few individuals: it becomes an overwhelmingly pervasive social problem. In most of the celebrated cases in the past, it was the principle of the matter that was at stake. At most, the question affected an individual here or a single family there. This is obviously true in regard to the most celebrated of these cases, those of Brother Daniel and Benjamin Shalit. Most of the other cases involved small communities, such as the Bnei Yisrael group from India and more recently the Ethiopian immigrants and more specifically the Falashmura.[19]

If we estimate the number of non-Jews among the Russian immigrants at a compromise figure of 20 or 25 percent, this translates into 150,000 to 200,000 individuals. Israel as a collective Jewish society has never faced a challenge in which so many non-Jews have gained entrance and demand equal treatment. In the past, secular arguments rested upon cosmopolitan liberal principles related to individual rights and freedoms. In response, the Orthodox leadership could cite Jewish continuity and integrality and insist that the area of "personal status"—of which the question of one's Jewishness is a defining part—was a do-or-die issue for them. Given its largely theoretical character, the secular community could acquiesce. Today, by contrast, the religious establishment faces a problem of such magnitude that the clever and accommodating compromise solutions of the past are powerless to resolve it.

Intolerable difficulties arise in a host of different areas. First of all, the presence of many non-Jews among the immigrants raises critical questions in regard to burial. Until the 1990s, the Orthodox rabbinate enjoyed exclusive and virtually total control over burial. The local religious councils together with the *chevra kadisha* (voluntary religious bodies that deal with preparing the deceased for burial) were basically unchallenged in their supervision of burial. The immigrants, however, create an unprecedented problem. According to Jewish law, non-Jews are not to be buried in Jewish cemeteries. Given the large number of non-Jews and the high percentage of aged immigrants, an explosion was inevitable. Published reports told of bodies that awaited burial for an unconscionably long period because the questionable Jewishness of the deceased prevented burial in the normal fashion. (It should be emphasized that Halacha itself relates to such practices as a dishonoring of the dead.) In a number of cases, bodies of "questionable Jews" were buried in special cemetery areas, quite distant from Jewish burial sites. In others, the bodies were buried outside of the cemetery altogether. These cases sparked strong public expressions of indignation. Most galling was the death of IDF soldiers, some of them in the line of duty, whose Jewish ancestries were challenged. Not surprisingly, the question of their burial (or nonburial) turned into an ugly public issue.

In 1995, the Sephardic Chief Rabbi Bakshi-Doron declared that "there is no escaping the need to establish alternative burial" in Israel. Moreover, the Chief Rabbinate announced that it would no longer oppose the creation of "secular cemeteries." In the mid-1990s, under the Labor Party government, it was decided that areas would be set aside for secular or civil cemeteries, in which anyone who wished could be buried—including Jews.[20]

On its face, this would seem to be a workable consociational resolution to the problem. Demographic changes made it clear to the religious community that a solution to the problem must be found; and in the event, it was accepted with few reservations. Yet, more closely scrutinized, this novel reality underscores—certainly in religious and particularly in Haredi eyes—the growing incompatibility of secular and religious Israel. They see Israel moving closer and closer to being just another state, without meaningful Jewish attributes. It is sloughing off its Jewish values apace, and, hence, the Haredim feel, they have no place in it. Secular burial may, in fact, be necessary, given the pressing demographic problem, but its deeper meaning is that the Law of Return, with its open-door policy to non-Jews, reflects secular Western as opposed to authentically Jewish loyalties. Under the title, "A Jewish Minority in Israel," one Haredi journalist mocks the secular world: "Only now, when you are drowning in goyim *[hegihu goyim ad nafesh]*, have secular leaders in Israel begun to understand the dangers of the 'Who is a Jew?' law in its secular version. . . . It threatens the existence of the State of Israel as a state of the Jews"—which is to say that although secular cemeteries may be practically unavoidable, the solution, grudgingly accepted, means that the Jewish partnership between the secular and religious communities becomes more and more tenuous.[21]

Resolving the burial issue is relatively simple in comparison with other critical issue areas. Regarding burial, there is maneuvering room for a compromise that does not grievously injure either side. Although secular cemeteries are anathema for the religious, it is, in general, a relatively minor concern. Their community is not directly compromised by their existence. The same is not true in regard to issues of "personal status," such as marriage and divorce. Here we confront the religious-secular standoff in its most intense and principled form. The salience of this issue derives, inter alia, from its being among the few areas in which a primary law (as opposed to secondary or local statutes) expressly and exclusively provides for total Orthodox control. The law says flatly that marriages and divorces "are to be conducted according to Torah law." For the religious, this critical provision keeps the Jewish people united, at least in regard to basic questions such as who is married in the eyes of the law and who is not. Without it, within a very few generations, the religious would be barred from marrying anyone outside their own community. Two different peoples, legally barred from conjugally mixing with one another, would come to be.

Even more pressing is the issue of *psulei chitun*, those who cannot be married in a Jewish ceremony—most often (but not exclusively) because they are the offspring of an adulterous relationship and deemed halachically to be bastards. Because the only form of marriage in Israel is religious, and because civil marriage does not exist, they are, in effect, barred from marrying—except with another *psul chitun*. Nothing like this issue exists in any other Western democracy. Alternatives to religious marriage, such as being married civilly in neighboring Cyprus, are usually the favored solution. Although it was always a particularly sensitive and charged issue, it never developed into a severe crisis because the numbers of those affected was rather small.[22]

That is, until the recent wave of immigration from the former Soviet Union transformed the reality dramatically. Awareness of the severity of the problem grew with the appointment of Shimon Shitrit of the Labor Party as minister of religion in 1995. Previously, the Ministry of Religion had always been in religious hands. This was the first time a nonreligious (although he defined himself as a traditional) Jew had served as minister. (The appointment was made after Shas broke with the Rabin coalition, creating a virtually unprecedented reality: an Israeli government without religious parties.) Shitrit made it clear early on that he intended to make sweeping reforms in the ministry, including the appointment of women to the religious councils, the introduction of "good government" criteria to the operation of the ministry, and so on. One of the central planks in his platform was to somehow resolve, or at least reduce to a minimum, the problem of psulei chitun. He was also bent on introducing a set of clear criteria that would, henceforth, serve to manage the issue rationally.

Shitrit, during the early months of his work on the subject, estimated that among the new immigrants the number of psulei chitun could easily reach one hundred thousand within a few years. Against the background of this dismaying estimation there was heard a growing chorus of voices from the non-Orthodox movements, the secular community, and the like that insisted on breaking the prevailing Orthodox monopoly and introducing the option of civil marriage in Israel. Shitrit did not go so far in his recommendations. He proposed, instead, that the "Cyprus option" be institutionalized and sanctioned by the state. He suggested that the state cover the expenses of the Cyprus trip for psulei chitun. Shas responded immediately that it would call for a no-confidence vote if this scheme were executed. One of the Shas members of the Knesset (Shlomo Benizry) demanded that the attorney general investigate Shitrit because, as a minister in the government, he was encouraging policies the object of which was evasion of the law of the land. Shitrit's suggestion was never adopted, and the problem of psulei chitun became increasingly more acute.[23]

From a relatively minor (if deeply distressing) issue, psulei chitun became an imposing social problem that affected tens of thousands. However, psulei chitun is just one relatively small aspect of a far larger problem catalyzed by the recent wave of immigration. Because religious marriage is the only kind of Israeli marriage, interreligious marriages cannot, ipso facto, take place. Unless one of the parties is willing to convert to the spouse's religion, there can be no marriage. Until the late 1980s this situation affected only small numbers of Israelis—Arabs and Jews—who wished to marry across religious lines. Today it has become an unavoidable and rampant problem. Those immigrants whose Jewishness is halachically questionable are simply marooned and without recourse in Israel. If they think of themselves as Jews and the prospective spouse is Jewish, their only option is to go through the tortuous process of conversion. Because, overwhelmingly, they are not Christians or Muslims, they cannot be married by a priest or *kadi*. Only the Cyprus option is possible.

For most adult immigrants this problem is not directly pertinent because the greater part of them were already married when they came to Israel (and Israel recognizes marriages performed abroad even if they are not religious). For the younger generation currently coming to marriageable age who are the offspring of a foreign marriage in which the mother's Jewishness is either questionable or clearly lacking, the dilemma looms large. One need not be clairvoyant to see that this is a time bomb that will explode when the problem becomes too large to be dealt with in clever or devious ways. If a hundred thousand nonmarriageable individuals suffer under the Orthodox monopoly, a hundred thousand potential spouses also suffer. When the impact on their families and friends is factored in, the problem encompasses virtually the entire community of recent immigrants. Minor consociational accommodations can no longer work—even if the will to pursue them is present. Although it is difficult to predict the outcome, it becomes progressively clearer that what was cannot continue to be. The Orthodox monopoly in marriage and divorce and the absence of civil marriage—perhaps the single most significant element in the consociational edifice of the past—appears to be doomed, at least in its present form.[24]

Some sense of the situation's urgency is captured in the dramatic surge in the sheer quantity of cases that are utterly intractable. For example, a couple, one of whom is halachically not Jewish, marries abroad in a civil ceremony. They come to Israel and now wish to divorce. Because there is no civil divorce in Israel, and the rabbinic courts do not deal with mixed couples, if the couple cannot (or will not) return to their home country to go through the divorce procedure, they are hopelessly stranded. Another typical example involves a Jewish woman married abroad in a civil ceremony to a Jew. She separates from her husband, even divorces him civilly. She now remarries civilly. There is the substantial fear that the rabbinate will recognize her first civil marriage and decide that because the couple lived together in a de facto marriage, a religious divorce is now required. In this case, the offspring of the second marriage will likely be deemed bastards and, hence, psulei chitun. Cases such as these come to the desk of Israel's attorney general in search of a solution. Until the early 1990s the number of such intractable cases that had accumulated in the attorney general's office ran between one hundred and two hundred per year. The number has soared more than tenfold—to more than two thousand cases at present.

In July 1998, a bill that would allow the marriage of "mixed couples" (but not psulei chitun) in Israel's family courts passed a preliminary reading. The bill was proposed, not surprisingly, by Roman Bronfman, a member of the Israel Be'aliya Party (the "Russian" immigrants' party). Although the bill is still at the early stages of legislation, it seems, in the complexity of its reception, to portend the shape of things to come.

At first blush, it would seem that the secular-religious divide would determine support and opposition to the law. Yet some leading parliamentarians related to the bill in quite unexpected ways. For example, one Haredi member of the Knesset (Moshe Gafni) remarked,

We are aware that there is a population with a problem that needs solving. The fact is that I [deliberately] was not present at the vote and that we [the Haredi parties] did not oppose the law or attempt to bury it at this stage. Were a similar law proposed by Meretz, I would not even read it. But in regard to Israel

Be'aliya everything we do is marked by discussion and agreement. I want to try and see how far we go with this law in the framework of Halacha.[25]

Recognizing the severity and urgency of the problem, the Haredi representative was attempting, defensively, to find consociational solutions. Although it is difficult to see how civil marriage can be made to fit into the halachic framework, the conciliatory tone reflects the Haredi recognition that change is mandatory.

Oddly, Roman Bronfman himself has been savaged by the secular and Russian press on grounds that his proposal releases the Haredim from responsibility. Strikingly, leading personalities of the secular Meretz Party opposed the bill. One of their number (Dedi Zucker) explained his position as follows:

Were it a matter of a third [final and decisive] reading and not a preliminary reading, I would have voted against Bronfman's bill. In the preliminary stage as well the vote is a signal to the Haredim that our strength is sapped [that is, they are ready to accept a compromise solution]. Bronfman's solution shifts the quantitative and qualitative pressure away from the rabbinate, while we have an interest that [the rabbinate] collapse under the strain—until they find a sweeping solution that recognizes civil marriage.[26]

In other words, now, under great pressure, the Haredim are willing to accept compromises that they rejected in the past—before the problem became so acute. Meretz, for their part, are not interested in patching or repairing an unacceptable state of affairs: consociationalism is no longer a viable option.

It might be argued that Bronfman's bill exemplifies the classic qualities of consociationalism. It is flexible, partial, and practical and attempts to toe a prudent line between the two adversaries. More carefully scrutinized, however, it appears in a very different light. In effect, the bill fails to encourage the minimal civility that is the hallmark of consociationalism; it does not moderate the intensity of the clash. It fosters rather than diminishes the distance and hostility between the camps and intensifies the sense of irreparable rupture and malice. From the Haredi point of view, the bill is merely another nail in the coffin of Jewish Israel, a compromise that is as hateful as it is exigent. A bill like Bronfman's, they might say, is prudent and realistic, but it is prudence coerced upon them by a deformed reality. It becomes necessary only because the Zionist reality is perverted and alien to the Jewish tradition. Zionist secularism, they contend, here displays its true colors: intermarriage condoned by the Jewish state.

Indeed, the Haredi community has begun to seriously consider the initiation of a genealogy register *(pinkas yuchsin)*[27] to keep track of who really is a Jew—which means, in effect, the creation of two kinds of Jews: those who are listed in the register, with whom they may mingle and marry, and those who are not. More accurately, for the Haredim those not included would not be considered Jews at all.

Beyond the deep antagonisms that a bill such as this arouses, it is also clear to the Haredim that, regarding civil marriage, at least, they face a steep and slippery slope. Once civil marriage is allowed in one case, there is precious little to stop it becoming an option open to all. They understand that it is only active public intervention in personal choice that prevents a deluge of demands for civil marriage. There is no more portentous or elucidating statistic in this regard than the one that reports on the number of couples that register with the rabbinate for marriage. Despite the precipitous growth in the Israeli Jewish population in the past decades, the number of those registering for religious marriage has remained unchanged since the late 1960s.

Conversion would seem to be the logical answer to the problem of newly arrived non-Jews; but the conversion issue is itself an intricate and intractable problem. Not only do many secular immigrants resist the idea of conversion as a matter of principle, the religious community itself is deeply divided between those who urge a relatively lenient and quick conversion and the conservatives who insist on the letter of the law, which means long and demanding conversions from which a great many potential converts would, in the end, be disqualified.

At stake is the question of intent. For the conservatives, a potential convert who does not, in good faith, take it upon himself or herself to live a religious life and observe all the commandments should not be accepted as a Jew. Because it is clear that the vast majority of non-Jews from the former Soviet Union do not so intend, their conversion is, for the conservatives, a mere sham. For the more liberal, by contrast, one need not enter into the concealed intentions of potential converts or demand the impossible.[28] Not surprisingly, the line between conservatives and liberals overlaps generally with the divide between the Haredim and the national religious community, and it is the potential converts who suffer from the infighting between them.[29] One editorialist in *Vesty* describes the conversion scene in Israel as totally unsatisfactory. There are too few "conversion programs" in existence. Even more galling are reports of a dismissive attitude on the part of the converting rabbis. The immigrants will often interpret "the attitude of the rabbinic courts as negative, at times as true hatred toward them."[30] It is clear, then, that salvation for those who find themselves in intractable positions will not come from the direction of conversion.

In sum, the difficulties facing the new immigrants are both qualitatively and quantitatively more radical than anything in Israel's history. They render the shrewd, discreet, and deliberately ambiguous accommodations of the past woefully inadequate. It becomes increasingly evident that without a radical solution, dire consequences will follow. Radical solutions, however, lead inevitably toward some form of civil marriage and the shattering of Orthodox dominance. This, in turn, entails the profound alienation of the religious communities from the Israeli collectivity—and so on in a vicious and destructive circle.

The Reform and Conservative Movements: Consociational Democracy and Religious Pluralism

The non-Orthodox movements—Conservative and Reform—were never a part of the consociational arrangements that regulated religious-secular relations in Israel. One observer notes that the uniqueness of the accommodational practices adopted in Israel lies in the fact that they only systematized the relations between the Orthodox and the nonreligious communities. As with many other issue areas (such as the left-right divide or the split between Arabs and Jews), religious pluralism was never a part of the complex system of compromises and arrangements that governed Orthodox-secular relations.[31] Part of the reason relates, no doubt, to the very small number of Conservative and Reform Jews in Israel. Estimates place their combined number at about fifteen thousand.

Despite their vast power in the Diaspora, the liberal wings of Judaism are repudiated by Israel's Orthodox rabbinical establishment without qualification or hesitation. A number of illustrations will suffice. During the High Holiday period, the religious council of Jerusalem regularly warns the public not to take part in non-Orthodox services. The omnipresent posters make it clear that frequenting a Conservative or Reform synagogue is worse than wasting one's time because these services do not acquit one of one's religious responsibilities, indeed they are, in themselves, an affront to Judaism and to God.[32]

Interestingly, the religious establishment makes it eminently clear that they have far greater a quarrel with the non-Orthodox streams than with the secular community. With secular Jews, so say the Orthodox spokespersons, at least one knows where one stands. The Conservatives and Reform, far more dangerously, claim to be speaking in an authentically Jewish idiom. If the secular are merely wayward, Conservative and Reform Jews are out-and-out usurpers.

Hence, the intensity and brutality of expression toward the non-Orthodox—especially in Haredi publications: "Christianity without a cross," "Do-it-yourself religion," "Rabbis without faith, educators without Judaism," and so on. One is not permitted to mingle with them ("asurim lavoh bakahal"). They are "the Hellenizers [mityavnim] of our time who fight to uproot everything."[33] Less fractiously but essentially in the same spirit, the Ashkenazi Chief Rabbi, Rabbi Israel Meyer Lau—a moderate, centrist, and representative figure in the religious community—comments at length:

We never had a problem with the Jewishness of Jews who were not observant. . . . I have no problem with someone who defines himself as secular. I do have a problem with someone who comes and says, "This we don't need, that is outmoded, and the other is anachronistic." He who changes something he did not create, he who comes to edit, to classify and differentiate—in crude language . . . to make a selection among the six hundred and thirteen mitzvot [commandments] and say this we need, that we don't need, this is relevant and that is not—and all of this under the aegis of halachic decision making and rabbinical, spiritual leadership, with this I do expressly have a problem. . . . You can come and tell me that I do not observe the Sabbath, my Sabbath is not the one described in Halacha—but I do not attempt to set up a different Halacha. . . . And I'm not even talking about the offense this commits against the great sages of Israel through the generations. On the subject of pluralism, I tell you the truth. Perhaps it is unpopular . . . but I do not see pluralism as an overriding value.[34]

It is against this background of uncompromising rejection that the drama involving the Orthodox, the non-Orthodox, the courts, and the political system unfolded in the late 1980s and early 1990s. The Reform and Conservative movements struggled for recognition in Israeli public life in regard to marriage and divorce, membership in religious councils, and, most especially, in matters of conversion.

Nevertheless, their efforts were selective. Because the Orthodox monopoly on marriage and divorce is explicitly enunciated in law and because the Reform and Conservative movements have little political power (apart from the support of Meretz), there are few options available to them in this regard except for public campaigns and appeals to the Supreme Court; and so they have turned, instead, to the issue of conversion. Here the law is ambiguous, and there is no provision that grants Orthodox exclusiveness. Even the 1970 amendment to the Law of Return that defined a Jew as one who was born of a Jewish mother and is not a member of another faith or has converted to Judaism does not specify what kind of conversion is acceptable. There is no delegation of hegemony to the Orthodox in the matter of conversion, as there is in the marriage and divorce bill. Indeed, despite a number of attempts by the religious parties to emend the law and introduce the phrase, "converted according to Halacha," they were consistently rebuffed by the Knesset—largely out of fear that the change would cause a serious break with the Diaspora, especially with Jews in the United States.

The status quo arrangement that developed over time was that conversions made abroad—even if they were Reform or Conservative—would be recognized by the Ministry of the Interior. By contrast, a conversion undergone in Israel would be recognized only if it were Orthodox. That is, Conservative and Reform conversions carried out in Israel would not be honored. This state of affairs was based, it should be emphasized, on precedent rather than on written law. Hence, the offensive of the Reform and Conservative movements zeroed in on this weak link; they appealed to the Supreme Court to have their own Israeli conversions recognized in Israeli law.

The religious parties, aware of the liberal and Western character of the Barak court, feared that the court's decision would not be in their favor. The court, for its part, was unhappy about being called upon to arbitrate this highly political issue; they would have preferred to have it addressed by the more political branches of the government. Still, it was clear that in the absence of political resolution or if the other branches of government tarried, the court would need to make its own ruling.

Against this background, the religious parties demanded that the Knesset legislate a "conversion bill" (known in Hebrew as the Chok Ha'hamara) to clarify once and for all that only Orthodox conversions would be recognized in Israel. Practically speaking, they wished to add the issue of conversion to the jurisdiction of the rabbinic courts and in so doing to ensure that it was under absolute Orthodox control. This would have placed conversion in a position similar to those of marriage and divorce.

The bill introduced at the beginning of 1997 created a veritable storm in Israeli public life as well as in many Jewish communities in the Diaspora. Spokespersons of the non-Orthodox movements made it quite clear that the passage of such legislation would mean an absolute break between their communities and the Jewish state. Among these voices there were those who demanded the end of all philanthropic activity on Israel's behalf, even working against Israel in the American Congress. Although it may be unclear how real these threats were, it is obvious that this might well have betokened a momentous transformation in Israeli relations with the Diaspora, especially with American Jewry.

These considerations led to a dangerous paralysis. On the one hand, passing the conversion bill might well precipitate a full-scale collision with American Jewry—with the Israeli secular community supporting the Reform and Conservative movements in the United States just as American Orthodoxy would support their Orthodox comrades in Israel. On the other hand, desisting from any decision would compel the Israeli Supreme Court to pronounce its verdict, one that the Orthodox feared would not be in their favor. It requires little imagination to grasp how incendiary such a decision would be, how many ultimatums would follow, how many threats to leave the ruling coalition would be voiced. Moreover, the Supreme Court would find itself in the eye of the public storm, and its future might well be imperiled. Whether the conversion law passed or not, what we have called the crisis-dominated (as opposed to consociational) nature of Israeli politics would be dramatically played out.

Because of this "damned if you do, damned if you don't" reality, in 1997 the government, in the hope of moderating the conflict and finding a compromise solution, set up the Ne'eman Commission to deal with the problem. The commission's establishment made for a freeze on all the legislative initiatives related to the conversion law as well as on all pending appeals to the Supreme Court. The commission presented its conclusions to the government at the start of 1998. The compromise that had been hammered out in marathon sessions was as follows: Conversion itself would be under the aegis of the Chief Rabbinate, which is to say, Orthodox. Yet the study of Judaism that would lead up to the conversion would take place in institutes in which instructors from all the

religious streams would be represented. The Knesset approved the commission's recommendations with an overwhelming majority, which included members from both the government and the opposition—seemingly a typical consociational solution. The Orthodox preserved their
monopoly in regard to conversion while the Conservative and Reform
movements gained unprecedented recognition in Israeli law.

The reality, however, turned out very differently. The Haredim expressed uncompromising opposition to the recommendations. In a public announcement, the Torah scholars of the Haredi camp called upon
their followers "to prevent the terrible desecration of God [hilul hashem]
involved in recognizing the Conservatives and the Reform and do all they
could to prevent this compromise. Anyone who lends his hand to these
criminals is counted among the enemies of God."[35] This Haredi root-
and-branch opposition is especially striking given that the commission's
recommendation leaves the actual conversion in the hands of the Orthodox rabbinate. The Chief Rabbinate found itself, as it so often did, in
an impossible mediate position, in a dilemma without resolution. This
dilemma appears to be intrinsic to the very nature of the established rabbinate. On the one hand, it is the country's official rabbinic leadership,
which serves a large majority of nonreligious Jews. On the other, it is
part of the Torah world and, as such, very sensitive to the authoritative
pronouncements of the Haredi rabbinic leadership.[36] In this case, the
Haredi leadership was far the stronger force, and the Chief Rabbis rejected the compromise solution because it involved the recognition of
non-Orthodox movements.

Opposition to the Ne'eman Commission's recommendations came
not only from the religious side; there were also those secularists who
expressed disappointment with the fact that conversion would remain
exclusively in Orthodox hands.[37] Knesset member Alex Lubotsky, one
of the shrewdest and most dedicated seekers of a compromise solution,
put his finger on the heart of the problem: The majority, he argues, supports the compromise. As to the Haredi minority who opposed it, he
states that "the time has come to push the extremists aside."[38] This is
precisely the problem: how, given the balanced two-camp system and
the dramatic growth of the Haredi representation, can this be done?[39]

In the summer of 1999 this tense political dead end gives no sign of
slackening. The commission's recommendations are suspended in midair.
On the one hand, the Orthodox have not backed down from their fervent opposition to the Ne'eman Commission's recommendations. On the

other hand, the Conservative and Reform appeals to the Supreme Court are still pending. Nor has the threat of passing a conversion law in the Orthodox spirit been removed. As in so many of the cases we have dealt with, the compromise solution languishes while the more radical alternatives—alternatives that would precipitate profound crises of legitimacy—threaten to materialize.

Chapter Six

The Future of Consociationalism

Judging by all we have written to this point, the future of consociationalism appears bleak, indeed. So many forces conspire against it, forcing retreat after retreat, that eulogies would seem more in place than analyses. It is precisely this summary conclusion that we would like to caution against. Consociationalism, though battered and weakened, is still a formidable presence in Israeli public life. Although the forces undermining consociationalism appear considerably more potent than those supporting it, the struggle between them has yet to be decided. The possibility that consociationalism will make a significant comeback—if for no other reason than the win-or-lose style creates unmanageable crises—should not be lightly dismissed.

This residual power of consociationalism requires explanation, and to offer such an explanation we need to take stock of our argument to this point. We began with a detailed presentation of consociational democracy, its character and the conditions that favor its emergence (chapter 1). It functions, we noted, to moderate conflict in the face of deep social, ideological, or religious cleavages by encouraging mutual adjustment, compromise, and accommodation. When it succeeds, consociational arrangements encourage the peaceable resolution of what would otherwise be difficult if not fatal confrontations. From the theory, we went on to the actual practice of consociationalism between the secular majority and religious minority as it took form during the early decades of Israel's existence (chapter 2).

In the subsequent chapters we described and analyzed the forces undermining consociational accommodation in Israel. We argued that deep structural changes in Israel's political life and in the dynamic of party competition were sapping the strength of consociationalism (chapter 3). We discussed the movement from a dominant-party to a balanced two-camp system; the rise of the Haredi parties and their "scale-tipping" power; the growing dominance of the Haredi over the National Religious Party—which became, unprecedentedly, a minority within the religious bloc; and finally, the dramatic convergence of religiosity with hawkish political views (and secularism with dovish views), which amounted to the decline of crosscutting and the rise of overlapping cleavages in Israeli public life.

We went on to recount the striking changes that have taken place judicially and "constitutionally" and their subversive effect upon the traditional accommodations between religious and secular Israel (chapter 4): to wit, the constitutional revolution occasioned by the new Basic Law on Human Freedom and Dignity and the Basic Law on Freedom of Occupation; the sharp rise in judicial activism in the Supreme Court; and finally, the Basic Law on the Government and its provision for the direct election of the prime minister. The critical demographic changes occasioned by the massive immigration from the former Soviet Union was our next subject (chapter 5). We explored the host of urgent but insoluble problems that arose from the application of religious law to a large community to which such concerns are alien, even offensive. We also studied the growing Conservative and Reform movements and their attempt to introduce religious pluralism in Israel. Finally, we noted how much more difficult it is today to make the kind of dubious deals that in the past lubricated the wheels of Israeli government. The entrenchment of liberal notions of good government, the rise of an aggressive investigatory press, the establishment of dozens of new watchdog organizations—all of these make discreet deals in the proverbial smoke-filled room more unlikely and more hazardous.

What is common to all these cases is the absence of a viable solution. Whatever avenue is pursued, confrontation seems unavoidable. When solutions are possible, they involve heading in profoundly anticonsociational directions—for example, breaking the monopoly of the Orthodox that is the heart of Israeli consociationalism. The room for maneuvering and compromise has grown smaller and more inhospitable, the issues more principled and ultimate. Does it come as any surprise, then, that in survey after survey most Israelis (in the 60 percent range) identify religious-secular conflict as the most dangerous for the stability and unity of the country—more than twice those who chose the dove-hawk split?

Never before have large sections of Israel's political leadership declared openly that their objective is to nullify the status quo agreement. Nor has the issue of drafting yeshiva students to the army ever been so charged. Never has the Labor Party taken such a principled anti-Haredi stand on the matter. Never before has the challenge of a large secular immigration faced a rabbinate with so few options for solution.

Hence our central thesis: The consociational order is crumbling, and a crisis-dominated order is emerging in its place. There are those who believe that the accommodationist stage is already very much behind us and that the collision of cultures is a fait accompli.[1] Others, by contrast, although they are aware of the rise in tensions and bad blood, see this as another of the rough spots on the consociational odyssey—from which the consociational spirit will extricate itself as it always has in the past.[2] We have deliberately presented the reality as neither one nor the other. This is not yet another of consociationalism's travails that will surely be overcome, nor is it the full-blown Armageddon itself. The truth, we suspect, is somewhere between these positions. The depth and breadth of the transformations are such that if they go unchecked for very much longer, they may well render the situation irremediable.

Given all the opposing trends we have reported, what prevents us from contending simply that consociationalism is dead? We believe that many elements in Israeli politics, both substantive and rhetorical, continue to reflect the consociational style. The habits of a century are not quickly forgotten—particularly if the religious issue is the sole area in which consociationalism is operative in Israeli public life. Some notable illustrations: Although the status quo agreement is violated by both sides with increasing impunity, references to its authoritative normative position continue unabated. It seems to live a life of its own. Similarly, the rhetoric of "one people" seems to work overtime just as its reality becomes increasingly doubtful. Even the impassioned campaign to have Haredi yeshiva students serve in the army turns on the "one people" theme. "We are all Jews," says the billboard, "Haredim, too."

Notably, as well, right-wing opposition to the Oslo Peace Accords was couched in unmistakable consociational language: Do not, they appealed to the Rabin government, take such decisive actions when your majority is so slim. Wait until a national consensus is consolidated. (Much the same rhetoric of waiting for unity and not relying on slender majorities was used by the left against Menachem Begin during the Lebanese war.) It should be added that many leading personalities in the Labor camp continue to be plagued by this same (consociationally grounded) question: Should the peace process be based on substantial national agreement—which could take decades to achieve—or is it the prerogative of the majority, however slim, to put its political program into practice?

Although we cannot adduce any hard evidence, our sense is that the momentum and importance of consociationalism is felt more acutely by the country's political leadership than by its citizenry. The public—or at least certain segments of it—seems more battle ready, more winner-take-all in their attitudes, than their own leadership. It is the leaders who appear to understand how exorbitant the price that such confrontationist strategies inevitably exact. Were the popular surge of religious-secular animosity of the past years to take its spontaneous course unchecked by the caution of the political elites, we fear that Israeli public life would be even more discordant than it is today.

Nevertheless, were it only a matter of consociationalism's inertial power, we would not be so cautious about announcing its demise. Even historical momentum will grind to a halt if powerful forces do not continue to impel it forward; and such forces, although in a weakened state, still endure. They mitigate what otherwise would be a no-holds-barred religious-secular confrontation. Of these forces, none compare in significance with the cultural effect of Israeli traditionalism. The "traditional" category includes a large cohort of Israelis who either explicitly define themselves as such or whose behavior patterns identify them as traditional, whatever their self-definition may be.[3] This large but normally inarticulate group, which has been described as the "forgotten center,"[4] plays a key role in supporting what remains of the consociational edifice.

This center is forgotten in the sense of being overlooked by the perceptions that dominate Israeli public discourse. The media image, often adopted by academic social analysts, is familiar and insistent: There are two Jewish societies in Israel, the one religious, the other secular, and they glare at each other across an unbridgeable cultural chasm. Israel is portrayed as a country riven into two camps, religious and antireligious, with nary a third alternative to moderate the standoff. They each occupy distinct and incompatible worlds of moral axioms, ideological imperatives, and life patterns. The only question that appears to remain unresolved is whether coexistence and conciliation are possible or, for that matter, even desirable.

This two-culture image is fundamentally misleading, not to say dangerous. There are, in fact, three major cultural orientations and three major publics that can be distinguished within the broad setting of Israeli society. Moreover, the public that is ignored by the two-camp conception is, arguably, the largest and most important in Israeli society. Indeed, were the confrontation solely between the secular and religious communities, consociationalism would have been history long ago.

For the traditionals, Jewishness is not a form of Judaism; it focuses its concerns on history, culture, and ethnicity rather than upon religion per se. Seen from the perspective of rigorous halachic Judaism, traditionalism is a variety of secular identity, even though many of its sources and practices may overlap with those of Judaism. Inspired by the desire to preserve meaningful ties to the Jewish people and to Jewish history, many Jews turn to the Jewish heritage, to the practices contained in the Jewish religious tradition, and adopt them as their own. In this way, religion is transmuted into folkways, theology into cohesiveness-enhancing family observances, and Orthodox devotion into communal solidarity. Despite essential differences in motive and purpose, secular Jews of this kind share a great deal with those conventionally spoken of as religious—in terms of both practices and collective commitments to Jewish continuity.

This disjointed, intellectually incoherent, and motley public selectively observes religious rites without being concerned with their theological import or the halachic consistency of their actions. Hence, it is not difficult to understand why traditionalism is overlooked. Given its folk-religious, practice-centered, inarticulate character, it rarely justifies itself in principled, creative, to say nothing of rebellious, terms. There are no traditionalist manifestos, no traditionalist intellectuals, no traditionalist political parties. Neither is traditionalism ideologically outspoken or, indeed, even clearly determinate on the right-left continuum, as are religiosity and secularism. As widespread as traditional Jewishness may be, it tends to elude the ready categories of the analysts.

Neither—and this is of great importance for our purposes here—does traditionalism understand itself as presenting a combative alternative to Judaism in its dominant Orthodox mode. It does not distinguish itself in the Israeli public sphere by assaulting or even disparaging the regnant religious establishment. Traditionalism lives alongside Orthodoxy without attempting to displace or supersede it. The Orthodox tradition is the source from which they pick and choose their preferred observances. For them, religion *is* Orthodoxy, even though they choose not to be bound by its laws. Because tradition is their focus, its practitioners have little desire to break ranks with tradition and create a new form of Judaism—such as that created by Conservative and Reform Judaism. Unlike the socialist-egalitarian movements of the heroic age of Zionism that strove to create a "new Hebrew person"—a revolutionary, explicitly antireligious conception of the Jewish mission and of Jewish values—traditionalism is quite content to live in the prosaic world of communal solidarity and routine practice. It is to be found in the myriad quotidian observances and conventions that densely organize the texture of everyday Israeli life. Traditionalism, in a word, possesses the protean character of popular, ethnocultural folkways that derive from Orthodox religious sources, often utilizes religious symbols, practices, and language, and yet is fundamentally not a religious phenomenon. It is rather a form of national self-identification expressed through the immemorial language of the Jewish tradition.

Much of the latent support for consociational accommodation derives from these traditional sources. The traditionals are as much as saying, "I may not be rigorously observant, but it is important that someone is. I can go my own way in the knowledge that others remain loyal to and perpetuate the faith"—or, as the political philosopher Shlomo Avineri famously cracked, "The synagogue I don't go to is an Orthodox one."

Hence, traditionalists want Orthodoxy to be a significant presence in the Jewish state. As long as they can practice in their own way, they are comfortable, perhaps even content, to see Orthodoxy as the official and public representative of the Jewish faith. Ironically, the secular and religious protagonists carry out their vocal confrontation as if unaware of the existence of this large traditional community.

The traditionalist presence explains why large sections of the Israeli populace—somewhere between two and three times the number of those who are Orthodox—support religious legislation of various kinds. To take only a single example, support for the exclusiveness of Orthodox marriage—by roughly half the Israeli populace—rests upon such traditional sentiments. This traditional community mediates between religious and secular demands, legitimating compromise and underwriting the continuing Orthodox influence over Israeli public life. Hence, the future of consociationalism will be critically affected by the future of Israeli traditionalism.

Nor can it be forgotten that feelings of solidarity continue to be quite powerful in Israeli society. Decades of the siege mentality have created solid social bonds that are as difficult to overlook as they are easy to mobilize. Although religious-secular conflict strains these bonds, there can be no doubt that they remain robust and will act as an important counterweight to the powers of division and conflict.

For so long as the major religious actors were from the national religious camp—most especially before the "settlers" movement dominated the NRP ideologically—this sense of solidarity was powerful and natural. The secular and religious communities were not two distinct societies; they lived together, served in the army together, worked together. The ascendancy of the Haredi community has greatly weakened this sense of unity. For much of the secular community and, to a degree, even among the national religious community, the Haredim are interlopers and freeloaders who continue to relate to the state of Israel as if it were a foreign (that is, non-Jewish) government and they were still in exile. Solidarity, under such circumstances, is considerably more difficult to maintain.

Some of the consociational spirit is also visible in the Labor Party's efforts to reach the traditional and Sephardi populations—often one and the same thing. Even if one chooses to be cynical about the motivations prompting these efforts, it remains nonetheless true that much of the Israeli left today recognizes that without traditionalist and Sephardi support, its political future is quite dim. (When, in 1996, they did not actively court this vote, they lost among Israeli Jews by a 55 to 45 percent margin.) Waging a political campaign that emphasizes the left's secularism, its Western liberal orientation, and its Ashkenazi character is widely recognized to be politically suicidal. Any winning electoral coalition will need to include substantial numbers of traditionals and Sephardim. The Labor platform must, for its own electoral health, adopt a strategy that contains significant consociational elements, one that steers away from secular decisiveness.

Nor have the dangers of an all-out confrontation been lost on many of the leading members of both the religious and secular communities. For each major crisis that erupts, certain consociational-style solutions are proposed. They are not, to be sure, as respected as they once were, nor do they carry the day, as they so often did in the past, but still the old habits die hard. For example, when the Conversion Law threatened to set community against community in an especially ugly way, the Ne'eman Commission (which included, notably, Orthodox, Conservative, and Reform representatives) was established. It put forward a proposal that was vintage consociationalism: Although there would be a single conversion process that required the confirmation of the Orthodox rabbinate, studies in preparation for conversion would be conducted in conversion institutes in which teachers from all the movements would be represented. In the end, the proposal failed because of intense opposition of the Orthodox. Even the minister of labor's assault on shopping centers' being open on the Sabbath was not really sustained; after strong public disapproval, it was relegated to the back burner. Meetings of conciliation took place between Chief Justice Aharon Barak and the leadership of Shas. It should be noted, if only in passing, that one religious member of the Knesset, Alex Lubotsky (of The Third Way)—who surely deserves the title, "the last of the real consociationalists"—has made a career of proposing all manner of conciliatory, conflict-mitigating settlements for religious-secular strife.

In regard to the exemption of yeshiva students from military service, thoughtful members of the Haredi community itself warn against straining the rope beyond what it can bear. Some (like member of the Knesset Shlomo Benizry, of Shas) have proposed the establishment of Haredi army units that would suit military service to the special needs of Haredi recruits. Notably, even the bill introduced by the Labor Party leader, Ehud Barak, to end the current wholesale exemption of Haredi yeshiva students does not attempt to nullify the entire practice. The principle of exemption would continue, but it would now be limited to a certain reasonable number (seven hundred) of such students a year.

Many other consociational symptoms are scattered throughout Israeli public life. Meimad, the small moderate religious party, has an unmistakably consociational program. Within the National Religious Party itself there remains a substantial constituency that opposes both radicalization and the growing influence of rabbinical authorities in determining political policy. This significant group resists what it sees as religious coercion and remains committed to accommodation with the secular community. Notably, in the summer of 1998, the leader of the NRP (Yitzchak Halevi) declared himself against further religious legislation or coercion except in areas that are clearly critical to Jewish perpetuity, such as marriage and divorce and conversion. Even on Israel's left, the concern with what is called the Jewish bookshelf (the Jewish canon) has led to secular attempts to revive Jewish learning in the secular style. The Tzameret Commission, established to deal with the conflict surrounding motorized traffic on the Sabbath in Jerusalem, has issued a report that attempts to accommodate all sides of the problem.

Most important, however, of these enduring consociational tendencies is the broad, almost universal acceptance of the principle of communal autonomy. Despite our assessment that consociationalism is seriously, perhaps even fatally, compromised by recent developments, it remains true that in regard to the principle of communal autonomy, consociationalism continues to enjoy almost wall-to-wall support in Israel. If consociationalism is understood as a social compact to respect each community's autonomy, to provide the services necessary for each community's flourishing, then consociationalism has few enemies in Israel. Even in the most acrimonious confrontations between the religious and secular communities, the idea of dismantling the religious educational stream, serving nonkosher food in the army, or eliminating public support for religious services such as synagogues is rarely, if ever, mentioned. There is no coherent voice in Israeli politics that wishes to adopt American-style separation of church and state. At this level of communal autonomy, consociationalism has been decisively victorious. Israel is as fully consociational as any of the classic European models; and if communal autonomy were all that consociationalism required for its functioning, this study would not have been necessary.

Consociationalism has foundered in Israel mainly because religious issues are no longer merely religious issues that focus on communal autonomy. They now largely coincide with the dove-hawk, Western-liberal–versus–traditional-conservative divides, and this renders the confrontation incomparably more hostile. It has become a struggle over the very physical borders and cultural character of the state, a politics of Jewish identity. Religious divergence—especially Haredi "triumphalism," on the one hand, and growing Westernization, on the other—has transformed what was a struggle for communal autonomy into an essential and principled struggle over the essential character of the Jewish collective.

For the religious communities, the official introduction of religious pluralism, for example, would not be just a setback; it would constitute an intolerable blow to the identity of the Israeli Jewish collective. If such an eventuality does, in fact, transpire, and if it is concurrent with retreat from territory and the dismantling of settlements, in their eyes the Jewish state may lose whatever remaining legitimacy it possesses.

(We would note, parenthetically, that were such a scenario to occur, the national religious community would find itself in a more intense dilemma than the Haredim. Although giving up their political clout would not be easy, the Haredim have a long history of isolationism, and this is, very likely, the kind of communal strategy to which they would return. The national religious community, by contrast, has staked its very existence on participation in the Zionist project. Indeed, they understand the Zionist experience in explicitly religious categories. How they would react if the basic justifications for their century-old beliefs were thwarted is impossible to predict.)

To be sure, the status quo ante included a number of issues extending beyond communal needs, such as religious control of marriage and divorce and the question of who is a Jew, but these, as we have seen, either affected only a few individuals or were grudgingly accepted as unavoidable and were rationalized on the grounds that they defined the conditions for active membership and full participation of the religious camp in Israeli society—the essential requirement for Jewish continuity. However, when a Haredi minister tries to close shopping centers on the Sabbath despite the absence of any real Haredi interests, when the clear motive is remaking Israel into a religiously observant country, consociationalism is left far behind.

Consociationalism is failing. For every public act that supports consociationalism, there are ten that undermine it. Playing to win is gaining momentum and emotional passion is intensifying just as the search for conciliation and accommodation is losing its force and its creative powers. The more conflict turns on the questions of who will control the public, collective space and which version of Jewish identity will prevail, the more consociational accommodation becomes irrelevant to Israeli politics.

Still, it is important to emphasize that the anticonsociational thrust may be arrested, even reversed. There is no overwhelming determinism playing itself out here. Indeed, if the intensity of religious-secular strife threatens the country's very integrity, the forces of conciliation may reappear and regroup. Crisis situations make for a clearer appreciation of the price to be paid for all-out confrontation. Perhaps leaders of both camps, sensing what lies ahead, will begin to restrain the more belligerent in their own camp. A similar outcome could result from a truly shocking and tragic event, such as a political murder committed against the background of the religious-secular strife, which would bring home the recognition that there can be no real victors in such a struggle.

Why, then, have we chosen to concentrate on the anticonsociational tendencies? There are two main reasons: First, the disintegration of consociationalism is the major change currently taking place—a change that has not been treated systematically elsewhere. Second, we believe that despite the potential for reversal, the forces opposing consociationalism are at present considerably more powerful than those sustaining it. There does not seem to be a satisfactory consociationalist solution to the many problems we have examined in this book. To grant a legal right to civil marriage and divorce—and this is the direction in which developments seem to be taking us—will force much of the religious community to sunder critical ties with Israeli public life, ties that have been painstakingly established over the generations. If, on the other hand, civil marriage is not permitted, the problems of mixed marriages, psulei chitun, and the like will only fester and finally burst. The same is true of religious pluralism. If the right of the non-Orthodox to equal treatment is denied, the collision course with liberal Israelis, not to speak of the world Jewry, is set. Yet, if pluralism is officially sanctioned—and there seems to be some movement in the direction of breaking up the Orthodox monopoly in the matter of burial, the composition of religious councils, and Sabbath observance in the public sphere—substantial parts of the religious and especially the Haredi community will read themselves out of the Israeli Jewish collective.

This either-or logic is at its strongest in regard to the peace process. If it continues successfully, that is, if substantial withdrawals are negotiated and a Palestinian state takes the place of Jewish settlements, there will be many in the religious camp for whom this will betoken a crossing of "red lines," an intolerable de-Judaization of the state. There will, without doubt, be those for whom such action on the part of a Jewish state is nothing less than treason in the literal sense of the word—and we have already been tragically witness to what such feelings can motivate. It cannot be said too strongly that the assassination of Yitzchak Rabin was no mere political act; it expressed, albeit in a perverted way, a despair born of religious motives that was integrally related to the struggle over the collective identity of the Jewish collective in Israel.

If, on the other hand, the peace process fails—and religious opposition to it will surely be one of the central reasons for such a failure—

equal and opposite reactions might well eventuate. Although the Israeli left has been far less given to violence than the right—the "Jewish underground," Baruch Goldstein, Yigal Amir, and the murderer of Emile Greenzweig all fired bullets that went from right to left—it is not unthinkable that deep despair and resentment might change the shape of things to come. It will, at least, lead many to reassess their desire to continue living in the Jewish state. It should not be forgotten that, in a general way unrelated to religious issues, Israel is becoming an increasingly violent society. In a tense, deeply divided polity in which the state is perceived as illegitimate or even treasonous, there is simply no telling which straw will break the camel's back.

If such admonitions sound overly apprehensive, it may well be because the issues at stake today are familiar continuations of issues that have a long Israeli history. Disagreement on motorized transportation on the Sabbath goes back to the prestate era. Drafting yeshiva students has been on the public agenda for fifty years. The conversion bill is merely an extension of the "Who is a Jew?" issue. The demand of non-Orthodox Jews to be equally represented and funded is nothing new, either. They are easy to dismiss as "la plus ça change, la plus ça rest la même chose." Still, this study has been dedicated to the thesis that something qualitatively different has taken place in recent years; hence, the potential for destructive crises along the religious-secular divide is far greater than ever before.

At the beginning of the 1950s, Israel's first prime minister, David Ben-Gurion, met with Rabbi Avraham Yeshaiyahu Karlitz—better known as the Chazon Ish—the recognized leader of the Haredi camp. When the subject of who should defer to whom was raised, the religious to the secular or the secular to the religious, the rabbi cited the following Talmudic case: If there are two wagons coming at each other on a narrow road, which one has the right of way? He opined that it was the empty wagon that needed to defer to the loaded one. Because the religious wagon is loaded heavy with commandments and learning, whereas secularism has no real cargo to speak of, the conclusion is obvious.

This is not how Israel's political reality has unfolded. The two wagons learned to move along abreast of each other in relatively satisfactory ways. At times, to be sure, there was friction between them, occasionally even collision. The basic accommodationist agreement, however, prevailed, and the wagons continued to progress alongside each other.

In the 1990s, the two wagons seem to have lost the ability or, for that matter, the will to accommodate each other. They appear to be headed for an unprecedented collision. The language of consociational reciprocity, compromise, and mutual adjustment is quickly giving way to strident talk of total victory. All we can say in response to these alarming trends is that consociationalism as a resolution to religious-secular conflict served the country well for many years. It is true that consociationalism is neither elegant, nor streamlined, nor inspiring. It tends to be convoluted, even illogical and unattractive. But, we must ask, are there any alternatives to it?

Notes

Prologue

1. All translations are those of the authors.

2. Tom Segev, *1949: The First Israelis* (in Hebrew) (Jerusalem: Domino, 1984), 239.

3. Dedi Zucker and Ran Cohen of the Meretz Party, as well as Rabbi Moshe Ezri representing the Reform movement in Israel, have expressed serious reservations with the slogan. See Rami Chazut, "Dedi Zucker: Stop the Slogan to Stop the Ultra-Orthodox" (in Hebrew), *Yedioth Ahronoth*, 27 June 1997, 7.

4. Quoted in Daniel Ben-Simon, "Bad Students of Voltaire" (in Hebrew), *Ha'aretz*, 4 July 1997, B7.

5. *Ha'aretz*, 25 Dec. 1997, 4.

6. This is the impression one receives from Benyamin Neuberger's excellent book, *Religion, State, and Politics* (in Hebrew) (Tel Aviv: Open University Press, 1994). This is also the dominating perspective of Eliezer Don Yehiya's various studies, to which we refer below.

One   Religion and State in Israel

1. See B. R. Wilson, "Religion in Secular Society," in *Sociology of Religion*, ed. R. Robertson (Harmondsworth, Eng.: Penguin, 1969), 152–62; and P. L. Berger, *The Social Reality of Religion* (Harmondsworth, Eng.: Penguin, 1973), 131–71.

2. P. L. Berger, "A Market Model of the Analysis of Ecumenicity," *Social Research* 30 (spring 1963): 77–93.

3. S. N. Eisenstadt, *Revolution and the Transformation of Societies* (in Hebrew) (Jerusalem: Bialik Institute, 1984), 162–64.

4. See Yaacov Katz, *The Exit from the Ghetto* (in Hebrew) (Tel Aviv: Am Oved, 1986); Shmuel Ettinger, *The History of Israel in the Modern Age* (in Hebrew) (Tel Aviv: Dvir, 1969); David Vital, *The Zionist Revolution* (in Hebrew) (Tel Aviv: Am Oved, 1978), 1:29–47; and Ehud Luz, *Parallels Meet: Religion and Nationalism in the Early Zionist Movement, 1882–1904* (New York: Jewish Publication Society, 1988).

5. Katz, *Exit from the Ghetto*; Vital, *Zionist Revolution*, 1:29–47; Luz, *Parallels Meet*, 29–62.

6. Gavriel Motzkin, "A Sketch of the Struggle between Religion and State in Europe in the Nineteenth Century," in *Priesthood, Kingdom, and the Relationship between Religion and State in Israel and the Nations* (in Hebrew), ed. Y. Gafni and G. Motzkin (Jerusalem: Shazar Center, 1987), 229–54.

7. See Eliezer Schweid, "Currents in Contemporary Judaism" (in Hebrew), *S'kira Chodshit* (Sept. 1979): 3–14.

8. Moshe Samet, *Conflicts over the Institutionalization of Jewish Values in the State of Israel* (in Hebrew) (Jerusalem: Hebrew University, 1980), 39–49.

9. The term is Charles Liebman's, in "Neotraditional Developments among Orthodox Jews in Israel" (in Hebrew), *Megamot* 26 (1982): 231–39.

10. Ibid.

11. Zeev Lacquer, *The History of Zionism* (in Hebrew) (Jerusalem: Schocken, 1974), 464 f.; Eliezer Schweid, *Motherland and Destined Land* (in Hebrew) (Tel Aviv: Am Oved, 1979), 118 f.; Vital, *Zionist Revolution*, 1:15–27; and Luz, *Parallels Meet*, 29 ff., 173–256.

12. On the various forms of confrontation during the early years of statehood, see Yosef Shalmon, *Religion and Zionism: The First Confrontations* (in Hebrew) (Jerusalem: Zionist Library, 1990). On the confrontations in the Yishuv—prestatehood—period, see Menahem Friedman, *Religion and Society: The Orthodox Non-Zionists in the Land of Israel* (in Hebrew) (Jerusalem: Yad Izhak Ben Zvi, 1978).

13. See Dan Horowitz and Moshe Lissak, *The Origins of the Israeli Polity: Palestine under the Mandate* (Chicago: University of Chicago Press, 1978).

14. Dan Horowitz and Moshe Lissak, *Trouble in Utopia* (Albany: State University of New York Press, 1989).

15. Arend Lijphart, *The Politics of Accommodation* (Berkeley: University of California Press, 1968); Arend Lijphart, "Consociational Democracy," *World Politics* 21 (1969): 207–55; Arend Lijphart, *Democracy in Plural Societies* (New Haven: Yale University Press, 1977).

16. Much of this description of consociational politics relies upon Eliezer Don Yehiya's exhaustive study of consociationalism in the Israeli context, "Participation and Conflict between Political Camps: The Religious Camp, the Labor Party, and the Crisis of Education in Israel" (in Hebrew) (Ph.D. diss., Hebrew University, 1976).

17. The term was used by Member of Knesset Amnon Rubenstein.

18. In later work, Lijphart extends his research to include "consensus" democracies with a legal-constitutional basis for accommodation. See his *Democracies* (New Haven: Yale University Press, 1984), 21–36.

19. Don Yehiya, "Participation and Conflict," 1:342 ff.

20. These ideas are associated with the well-known research of Seymour Martin Lipset.

Two *Consociational Democracy in the First Generation*

1. This view has its academic supporters, as well. See Shmuel Sager, *The Parliamentary System of Israel* (in Hebrew) (Tel Aviv: Achiasaf, 1988), 226 (published in English under the same title [Syracuse: Syracuse University Press, 1985]); and Asher Arian, *Politics in Israel: The Second Generation* (Chatham, N.J.: Chatham House, 1989), 94–100.

2. See Eliezer Don Yehiya, "Participation and Conflict between Political Camps: The Religious Camp, the Labor Party, and the Crisis of Education in Israel" (in Hebrew) (Ph.D. diss., Hebrew University, 1976), 196–258.

3. Ofira Seliktar, "Coalitional Theories and the Making of Coalitions: Research on the Israeli Case," in *State, Government, and International Relations* (in Hebrew) 8 (Sept. 1975): 120.

4. See Zerah Wahrhaftig, *A Constitution for Israel: Religion and State* (in Hebrew) (Jerusalem: Mesilot, 1988), 34–36. This study is a valuable source for the many arrangements that developed in religion-state matters—from the perspective of one of the leaders of religious Zionism.

5. See Benyamin Neuberger, *Religion, State, and Politics* (in Hebrew) (Tel Aviv: Open University Press, 1994), 42–52; and Eliezer Don Yehiya, "The Resolution of Religious Conflicts in Israeli Politics," in *Conflict and Consensus in Jewish Political Life*, ed. Stuart Cohen and Eliezer Don Yehiya (Ramat Gan, Isr.: Bar-Ilan University Press, 1986), 203–18.

6. See Menahem Friedman, "And These Are the Chronicles of the Status Quo: Religion and State in Israel," in *The Transition from Yishuv to State, 1947–1949: Stability and Change* (in Hebrew), ed. V. Pilusvky (Haifa: Herzl Foundation for the Study of Zionism, 1988), 47–97.

7. See Benyamin Neuberger, *The Constitution Issue in Israel* (in Hebrew) (Tel Aviv: Open University Press, 1990), 7–21; and Ze'ev Segal, *Israeli Democracy* (in Hebrew) (Tel Aviv: Ministry of Defense, 1988), 22–28.

8. Arend Lijphart, *Democracies* (New Haven: Yale University Press, 1984), 21–36.

9. A full discussion of the various possible motives can be found in Neuberger, *Constitution Issue in Israel*, 22–37; Wahrhaftig, *A Constitution for Israel*, 76–85; and Daphne Sharfman, *Public Authority versus Individual Rights in Israel* (in Hebrew) (Haifa: Etika, 1997), 43–51.

10. *Divrei Haknesset*, 4:718, 729 ff., 811 ff.

11. See Wahrhaftig, *A Constitution for Israel*, 229–38.

12. See Friedman, "And These Are the Chronicles of the Status Quo," 47–97.

13. On the fear of "erosion," see Menahem Friedman, *Haredi Society* (in Hebrew) (Jerusalem: Institute for the Study of Israel, 1991), 52 ff.

14. Yechezkel Cohen, *Induction According to Halacha: On the Exemption*

of Yeshiva Students from the IDF (in Hebrew) (Jerusalem: Ne'emanay Torah Ve'Avoda, The Religious Kibbutz, 1993), 203–7.

15. On the legal aspect of the issue, see Menahem Hoffnung, *State Security versus the Rule of Law* (in Hebrew) (Jerusalem: Nevo, 1991), 244–48.

16. See Cohen, *Induction According to Halacha*, 244–48.

17. See Friedman, "And These Are the Chronicles of the Status Quo," 47–97.

18. See Gad Barzilai, *Democracy at War* (in Hebrew) (Tel Aviv: Sifriat Hapoalim, 1992), 14–20; and Dan Horowitz and Moshe Lissak, *Trouble in Utopia* (Albany: State University of New York Press, 1989), 240–47.

19. See Cohen, *Induction According to Halacha*, 203–7.

20. See Menahem Friedman, "The NRP in Flux: The Background to Their Electoral Decline" (in Hebrew), *Medina U'Mimshal Ve'yachasim Beynle'umiyim*, nos. 19–20 (1982): 105–22.

21. *Divrei Haknesset*, 2:1445–46.

22. See *Report of the Tenth Congress of the Ha'Poel Hamizrachi Association* (in Hebrew) (Jerusalem: Ha'Poel Hamizrachi Publishers, 1938), 261.

23. For an extensive description and analysis by one of the leaders of the religious Zionists, see Moshe Una, *In Separate Ways: The Religious Parties in Israel* (in Hebrew) (Alon Shvut-Gush Etzion, Isr.: Yad Shapira, 1984), 256–80. See also Wahrhaftig, *A Constitution for Israel*, 238–61.

24. Wahrhaftig, *A Constitution for Israel*, 264–65.

25. Cited ibid., 274.

26. On the allegation of police brutality in religious demonstrations, see Giora Goldberg and Sam Lehman-Wilzig, "Religious Protest and Police Reactions in a Theo-Democracy," in *Criminality and Social Deviance* (in Hebrew) 12 (1984): 23–31.

27. See Wahrhaftig, *A Constitution for Israel*, 271. On the limitations on leadership in religious parties, see Asher Cohen, *The Talit and the Flag: Religious Zionism and the Concept of a Torah State, 1947–1953* (in Hebrew) (Jerusalem: Yad Izhak Ben Tzvi, 1998), 89–136.

28. For a full discussion, see Don Yehiya, "Participation and Conflict."

29. *Divrei Haknesset* 4:884.

30. For a full analysis, see Tzvi Tzameret, *Melting-Pot Days* (in Hebrew) (Sde Boker, Isr.: Center for the Legacy of Ben-Gurion, 1993).

31. Tzvi Tzameret, *On a Narrow Bridge: Education in Israel's First Years* (in Hebrew) (Sde Boker, Isr.: Center for the Legacy of Ben-Gurion, 1997), 227.

32. See ibid., 240–42.

33. The responses are included in H. Regev, S. Meyer, and H. Shemesh, *Religion, Society, and State* (in Hebrew) (Jerusalem: Ministry of Education, 1987).

34. Neuberger, *Religion, State, and Politics*, 84–85.

35. On the legal developments in this area, see Amnon Rubenstein and Barak

Medina, *The Constitutional Law of the State of Israel* (in Hebrew) (Jerusalem: Schocken, 1996), 1:111–39.

36. On the formation of coalitions in the period of Mapai dominance, see Danny Koren and Boaz Shapira, *Coalitions* (in Hebrew) (Tel Aviv: Zmorah Bitan, 1997), 239–88, 376–83.

37. Giora Goldberg, *Political Parties in Israel: From Mass Parties to Electoral Parties* (in Hebrew) (Tel Aviv: Ramot, 1992), 26–28, 34–40.

Three   Old Issues, New Politics

1. For a general discussion, see Giora Goldberg, *Political Parties in Israel: From Mass Parties to Electoral Politics* (in Hebrew) (Tel Aviv: Ramot, 1992); and Benyamin Neuberger, *Political Parties in Israel* (in Hebrew) (Tel Aviv: Open University Press, 1997), 240–47.

2. A clear expression of this attitude can be seen in Member of Knesset Shevach Weiss's analysis of the election results. Its title says it all: *Where Were the Missing 14,900 Votes?* (in Hebrew) (Tel Aviv: Hakibutz Hameuchad, 1997).

3. Eliezer Don Yehiya, "Religious Leadership and Political Leadership," in *Spiritual Leadership in Israel* (in Hebrew), ed. Ella Belfer (Jerusalem: Institute for Judaism and Contemporary Thought, 1982), 104–34.

4. See Asher Cohen, *The Talit and the Flag: Religious Zionism and the Concept of a Torah State, 1947–53* (in Hebrew) (Jerusalem: Yad Izhak Ben Zvi, 1998).

5. See Menahem Rahat, "Confusion among the Politicians," *Ma'ariv,* 16 Apr. 1999, 2.

6. Expressions of outrage against religious "blackmail" fill the pages of Israel's print media regularly. They rise to an even higher level during the debates of the national budget and in the context of coalitional debates. These expressions of exasperation and anger were not heard in the first generation of statehood.

7. On the autonomy given to the religious camps, see Tzvi Tzameret, *On a Narrow Bridge: Education in Israel's First Years* (in Hebrew) (Sde Boker, Isr.: Center for the Legacy of Ben-Gurion, 1997).

8. Tamar Trebelsi-Haddad, "A Contended Appointment" (in Hebrew), *Yedioth Ahronoth, 24 Hours* (supp.), 5 Nov. 1997, 13.

9. For a blow-by-blow account, see Guy Bechor, *A Constitution for Israel: An Account of the Struggle* (in Hebrew) (Tel Aviv: Sifriat Ma'ariv, 1996), 127–54; and Gideon Alon, *Direct Election* (in Hebrew) (Tel Aviv: Bitan, 1995), 62–87.

10. On Barak's pronouncements, see Yael Gewirtz, "Barak: 'I Will Make Certain That the Haredim and the Arabs Will Be Drafted'" (in Hebrew),

Yedioth Ahronoth (Sabbath supp.), 5 Dec. 1997; for the Haredi response, see *Yedioth Ahronoth,* 7 Dec. 1997, 25, and *Ha'aretz,* 7 Dec. 1997, A4.

11. *Ha'aretz,* 5 Apr. 1998, A10.

12. Menachem Porush of Agudat Israel served as deputy minister between 1990 and 1992, but Ishay was the first full-fledged minister of labor and welfare from a Haredi party.

13. *Yedioth Ahronoth,* 9 Jan. 1998, 9; *Ha'aretz,* 11 Jan. 1998, A6, and 2 Mar. 1998, A4.

14. Editorial, *Ha'aretz,* 19 Dec. 1998, B1.

15. See, for example, the collected reports under the title "Sabbath Rows" (in Hebrew), *Ha'aretz,* 18 Jan. 1998, A2.

16. See chapter 5, this volume, for details.

17. Broadcast by Israeli radio (in Hebrew), channel 2, *Tofsim Keevun,* on 17 Jan. 1998.

18. Menahem Friedman, "From Erosion Trauma to Feelings of Confidence and Superiority" (in Hebrew), *Migvan* 63 (Sept. 1981): 9–14.

19. Quoted in Daniel Ben-Simon, "Infants of the Kratchnef House" (in Hebrew), *Ha'aretz,* 26 Dec. 1997, B7.

20. Ran Kislev, "The War Has Already Begun" (in Hebrew), *Ha'aretz,* 13 Jan. 1998, B1.

21. Amnon Dankner and Ron Miburg, "The End of the Entrecôte Season" (in Hebrew), *Ma'ariv* (Sabbath supp.), 9 Jan. 1998, 6–7.

22. Yechezkel Cohen, *Induction According to Halacha: On the Exemption of Yeshiva Students from the IDF* (in Hebrew) (Jerusalem: Ne'emanay Torah Ve'Avoda, The Religious Kibbutz, 1993), 89–100.

23. See Stuart A. Cohen, *The Scroll or the Sword?* (Amsterdam: Harwood Academic Publishers, 1997).

24. Much of Menahem Friedman's work is dedicated to exploring this proposition.

25. See Aryeh Bender and Etai Asher, "The Enraged Students On Strike: They Want Benefits like Those of the Yeshivot" (in Hebrew), *Ma'ariv,* 2 Jan. 1998, 4.

26. Apart from Rehavam Ze'evi, the other Moledet members of the Knesset have been Orthodox Jews from the national religious camp.

27. Charles Liebman, "The Religious Element in Israeli Nationalism" (in Hebrew), *Gesher* 113, no. 2 (1986): 63–78; Avner Horowitz, "Religious Zionism from Zionist Radicalism to Nationalist Zealotry," in *Religion and State in Israel,* ed. Donna Arieli-Horowitz (in Hebrew) (Jerusalem: Center for Jewish Pluralism of the Movement for Reform Judaism, 1996), 41–55.

28. Amnon Kapilyuk, *Rabin: Political Murder with the Help of God* (in Hebrew) (Tel Aviv: Sifriat Hapoalim, 1996); Moly Peleg, *To Spread the Wrath of God* (in Hebrew) (Tel Aviv: Hakibutz Hameuchad, 1997).

29. Shulamit Aloni, *The Arrangement: From a Law-Governed State to an Halachic State* (in Hebrew) (Tel Aviv: Otpaz, 1970).

30. For survey research data, see the "Peace Barometer" of the Tami Steinmetz Center for Peace Research, Tel Aviv University, "Secular, Ashkenazi, Rich, Seeking Peace" (in Hebrew), *Ha'aretz,* 7 Dec. 1997, B2, as well as *Religious-Secular Relationships in Israel* (in Hebrew) (Tel Aviv: Tami Steinmetz Center for Peace Research, Tel Aviv University, 1998), 61–72.

31. This despite the fact that survey data indicate that Haredi voters are, if anything more radical than NRP voters. See, for example, *Religious-Secular Relationships in Israel.*

32. See Menahem Friedman, "The First Non-Zionist Right" (in Hebrew), *Meimad* 7 (1996): 12–16.

33. Eliezer Don Yehiya, "Religiosity and Ethnicity in Israeli Politics" (in Hebrew), *Medina U'Mimshal Ve'yachasim Beynle'umiyim* 32 (1990): 1–47. See also his "Religion, Ethnicity, and Electoral Reform: The Religious Parties and the 1996 Elections," in *Israel at the Polls, 1996,* ed. Daniel J. Elazar and Shmuel Sandler (London: Frank Cass, 1998), 73–102.

34. Eliezer Don Yehiya, "Stability and Change in a Camp Party: The NRP and the Revolt of the Youth Wing" (in Hebrew), *Medina U'Mimshal Ve'yachasim Beynle'umiyim* 14 (1979): 25–52.

35. Hanah Kim, "The Third Sector" (in Hebrew), *Ha'aretz,* 13 Jan. 1998, B1.

36. Mordechei Gelat, "Beige Shochat: In Less than Ten Years, A Khoumeini-like State Is Liable to Arise Here" (in Hebrew), *Yedioth Ahronoth* (Sabbath supp.), 2 Jan. 1998, 14–15.

37. David Grossman, "In Favor of a Unity Government" (in Hebrew), *Yedioth Ahronoth, 24 Hours* (supp.), 19 May 1999, 5; Orit Shachat, "One Israel, and a Half" (in Hebrew), *Ha'aretz,* 20 May 1999, B1; Ron Miburg, "A Conciliatory Hand: Restraint Is Gold" (in Hebrew), *Ma'ariv,* 20 May 1999, 3; Dan Margalit, "Shas Is Not Leprous" (in Hebrew), *Ha'aretz,* 24 May 1999, B1; Avirma Golan, "A Time for Civility" (in Hebrew), *Ha'aretz,* 23 May 1999, B1.

Four   The Judicial and Constitutional Dimension

1. Benyamin Neuberger, *Religion, State, and Politics* (in Hebrew) (Tel Aviv: Open University Press, 1994), 51.

2. Gad Barzilai, Epi Yuchtman-Yaar, et al., *The Courts in the Public Eye* (in Hebrew) (Tel Aviv: Papyrus, 1994).

3. *Bagatz* (Supreme Court Rulings), *Shalit v Minister of the Interior,* 68/58, *Piskei Din* (Decisions) 24, at 2:477.

4. See Amnon Rubenstein and Barak Medina, *The Constitutional Law of the State of Israel* (in Hebrew), 5th ed. (Jerusalem: Schocken, 1991), 1:142–63.

5. Menaham Mautner, *The Decline of Formalism and the Rise of Values in Israeli Law* (in Hebrew) (Tel Aviv: Ma'galei Da'at, 1993), 101. See also his "Law as Culture: Toward a New Research Paradigm," in *Multiculturalism in a Jewish and Democratic State* (in Hebrew), ed. M. Mautner, Avraham Sagi, and R. Shamir (Tel Aviv: Ramot, 1998), 545–87.

6. As one leading jurist has described it, the activist approach is "more subjective than objective. It expresses the will of the judge to be involved, a tendency toward dominance, the desire to determine new forms of life, and the readiness to bear responsibility for the consequences of novelty." Yitzchak Zamir, "Judicial Activism: The Decision to Decide" (in Hebrew), *Eeyunei Mishpat* 17, no. 3 (Jan. 1993): 649.

7. *Bagatz, Bavli v The Supreme Rabbinical Court*, 1000/92, *Piskei Din* 48, at 2:221.

8. Cited by Menachem Alon, in "These Are Only Casual Statements . . . That Are in Error, and It Behooves Us to Abandon Them," in "Dissents and Reflection in the Wake of the Bavli Issue," in Mautner, Sagi, and Shamir, *Multiculturalism in a Jewish and Democratic State*, 363.

9. *Bagatz, Bavli v Supreme Rabbinical Court*, 243.

10. Ibid., 251–52.

11. This is one of six criteria in what is referred to as the canon model, the purpose of which is to measure the degree of judicial activism in a given legal system. See Aharon Barak, "The Essence of Judicial Activism: A World View Regarding Law and Adjudication" (in Hebrew), *Eeyunei Mishpat* 17, no. 3 (Jan. 1993): 4987–4999.

12. *Bagatz, Bavli v Supreme Rabbinical Court*, 375.

13. Barak, "The Essence of Judicial Activism," 485–87.

14. Ibid., 492.

15. See chapter 2, this volume.

16. *Bagatz, Ressler v the Minister of Defense*, 448/81, *Piskei Din* 36, at 1:88–89.

17. Ibid., 910/86, *Piskei Din* 42, at 2.

18. Different and not always consistent data is published about the number of yeshiva students not serving in the army. Still, there is no argument but that the number of deferred yeshiva students has grown significantly—not only in absolute numbers but also in proportion to those drafted each year. According to the data provided by the government in the 1996 trial, the number of deferments rose to 8.0 percent of the yearly draft, compared with 5.8 percent in 1993. See Shachar Ilan, "Sin and Its Reward" (in Hebrew), *Ha'aretz*, 26 May 1998, B2.

19. This position was expressed in large ads placed in all three of Israel's daily newspapers on 22 May 1998. On the solidarity of the Haredi world in this regard, see Menahem Rahat, "Rabbi Schach: There Is No Room for Negotia-

tion and Compromise in the Matter of the Draft for Yeshiva Students" (in Hebrew), *Ma'ariv,* 1 June 1998, 8.

20. Daliah Schori, "Chazan Wants the Attorney General to Start Proceedings against Rabbi Schach for Advocating Rebellion" (in Hebrew), *Ha'aretz,* 24 Sept. 1998, A8.

21. Menahem Rahat, "Two Hours without a Coalition" (in Hebrew), *Ma'ariv,* 28 January 1999, 1–3.

22. Shachar Ilan, "A Tour Of the Conversion Map" (in Hebrew), *Ha'aretz,* 7 June 1998, B2; Menahem Rahat et al., "The Conversion Law Splits the Coalition" (in Hebrew), *Ma'ariv,* 5 June 1998, 2. This issue is taken up more fully in chapter 5.

23. Aharon Barak, "The Judicial Revolution: The Protection of Basic Rights" (in Hebrew), *Mishpat U'mimshal* 1 (1992): 30–31.

24. See Shachar Ilan, "Hammer at the NRP's Convention: The Religious Community Feels Persecuted by the Supreme Court" (in Hebrew), *Ha'aretz,* 20 Sept. 1994, A5.

25. Yigal Bibi's remarks appeared prominently in all the daily papers on 11 June 1998.

26. Chief Justice Barak's assertions appeared in all the daily newspapers on 3 June 1998.

27. For extended analyses, see Guy Bechor, *A Constitution for Israel: An Account of the Struggle* (in Hebrew) (Tel Aviv: Sifriat Ma'ariv, 1996), and Gideon Alon, *Direct Election* (in Hebrew) (Tel Aviv: Bitan, 1995).

28. See Ze'ev Segal, *Israeli Democracy* (in Hebrew) (Tel Aviv: Ministry of Defense, 1988), 22–34.

29. For an exposition of the arguments against the activist reading, see Benyamin Neuberger, *The Constitution Issue in Israel* (in Hebrew) (Tel Aviv: Open University Press, 1990), 77–79.

30. Paragraph 10 of the Basic Law: Human Freedom and Dignity, *Sefer Chukim* (Law compendium), 90.

31. Yehudit Karp, "Basic Law: Human Freedom and Dignity—A Biography of Power Struggles" (in Hebrew), *Mishpat U'mimshal* 1 (1993): 342.

32. See David Kretzmer, "The New Basic Laws on Human Rights: A Mini-Revolution in Israeli Constitutional Law," *Israeli Law Review* 26, no. 2 (1992): 238–49.

33. For *Mitral*-related decisions, see *Bagatz, Piskei Din* 5781/92, 3872/93, 7198/93, and 5009/94.

34. See Karp, "Basic Law," 345–61.

35. See Ronen Tal, "The 'Lice' Speech of Judge Aligon" (in Hebrew), *Ma'ariv,* 28 Jan. 1999, 13; Shachar Ilan, "Anti-Semitic People in the Legal System Call Shas Supporters 'Lice,'" (in Hebrew), *Ha'aretz,* 2 Feb. 1999, A5.

36. See Shachar Ilan et al., "A Biting Haredi Attack on the Supreme Court:

Barak as Persecutor of the Jews" (in Hebrew), *Ha'aretz,* 10 Feb. 1999, A1; Shachar Ilan, "Rabbi Joseph: The Supreme Court Judges Are Evil Men" (in Hebrew), *Ha'aretz,* 11 Feb. 1999, A1.

37. Shlomo Tzasneh and Menahem Rahat, "The Haredim Have Declared War on the Supreme Court" (in Hebrew), *Ma'ariv,* 10 Feb. 1999, 1–3.

38. See Shmuel Mittelman, "An Appeal to the Supreme Court: To Direct Rubenstein to Put Ovadia Yosef on Trial" (in Hebrew), *Ma'ariv,* 1 Mar. 1999, 19.

39. Runel Fisher, "They Won't Take Me Alive" (in Hebrew), *Ma'ariv* (weekend ed.), 1 Mar. 1999, 8–12.

40. See Menahem Rahat, "Divisions in the NRP: The Rabbis Are with the Haredim, the Ministers Are 'on the Fence'" (in Hebrew), *Ma'ariv,* 15 Feb. 1999, 4; *Ha'zofeh,* 19 Feb. 1999, 2–6.

41. Eliyahu Swissa, "All of Shas Was on Trial" (in Hebrew), *Ma'ariv,* 18 Mar. 1999, 11.

42. See Alon, *Direct Election,* 62–86.

43. Bernard Susser, "The Direct Election of the Prime Minister: A Balance Sheet," in *Israel at the Polls, 1996,* ed. Daniel Elazar and Shmuel Sandler (London: Frank Cass, 1998), 237–57.

44. See Shalom Yerusahlmi, "Netanyahu's Shock Troops" (in Hebrew), *Ma'ariv* (Holiday supp.), 29 May 1998, 24–25.

45. See the discussion by Daniel Ben-Simon, *Another Country: The Victory of the Marginals—How the Left Collapsed* (in Hebrew) (Tel Aviv: Aryeh Nir, 1997).

Five   Demographic, Cultural, and Religious Changes

1. Davida Lachman-Meser, "The New Media Map in Israel: The Process, the Characteristics, and the Question Marks" (in Hebrew), *Dvarim Acherim* 1 (spring 1997): 66–87.

2. Its author was Shachar Ilan, the *Ha'aretz* reporter for religious affairs. The series began to appear in the second section of the paper in 1998. Most of the articles appeared between March and May.

3. See, for example, the articles for 17 Mar. 1998, 19 May 1998, and 26 May 1998.

4. See Asher Cohen, "On Nose Picking," *The Seventh Eye* (in Hebrew) 13 (Feb. 1998): 30–31.

5. Many such examples can be found in Dov Elboym, "The Garbage Brigade and the Drug Gluttons," *The Seventh Eye* (in Hebrew) 4 (July–Aug. 1996): 18–21.

6. See Shachar Ilan, "Rubenstein Warned the Editor of the Haredi Paper,

The Week, to Cease Publishing Libelous Material" (in Hebrew), *Ha'aretz*, 21 Nov. 1997, A6.

7. Ehud Sprintzak, *As You Like It: Illegalism in Israel Society* (in Hebrew) (Tel Aviv: Sifriat Hapoalim, 1986), 63–75.

8. Ephraim Tabory, "The Absorption of the Soviet Jews in Israel and Its Effect on Israeli Society" (in Hebrew), *Gesher* 37, no. 123 (1991): 7–20.

9. Giora Goldberg, *The Israeli Voter, 1992* (in Hebrew) (Jerusalem: Magnes, 1994), 203–4.

10. Tzvi Gittelman, "Jewish-Soviet Identity in a Period of Change," *Soviet Jews in Transition* (in Hebrew) 1, no. 16 (1994): 152. See also Elazar Leshem, "Judaism, Religious Lifestyle, and Positions Regarding Religion and State among Immigrants from the Former Soviet Union," in *Religion and State Yearbook: 1993–1994* (in Hebrew), ed. Avner Horowitz (Jerusalem: Center for Jewish Pluralism of the Movement for Reform Judaism, 1994), 36–53.

11. Alexandra Kateiba, "The Freedom to Choose" (in Hebrew), *Politika* 45 (1992): 37.

12. Shachar Ilan, "Religious Laws Will Collapse and Religion Will Be Separated from the State" (in Hebrew), *Ha'aretz*, 3 May 1995, B2.

13. Among other places, such confrontations took place in Ashdod, Ashkelon, and Migdal Ha'emek. See *Ha'aretz*, 3 Dec. 1997, B3; 16 Feb. 1998, A6; and 11 Mar. 1998, A1.

14. Raphael Nudelman, "In Search of Ourselves," *Soviet Jews in Transition* (in Hebrew) 3, no. 18 (1997): 20.

15. Data collected by David Sherman for a seminar paper, 1999, Department of Political Studies, Bar-Ilan University.

16. Uri Gordon, "And the Grandchildren Will Return to Their Boundaries" (in Hebrew), *Al Hamishmar*, 28 Aug. 1994.

17. Aharon Fine, "The Jewishness of Soviet Immigrants," in *The Immigration and Absorption of the Former Soviet Jews: A Bibliography* (in Hebrew), ed. Elazar Leshem and Dina Shor (Jerusalem: Henrietta Szold Institute, 1994), 145.

18. See, for example, Alex Somech, "A Decline in the Percentage of Jews among the Immigrants from the CIS" (in Hebrew), *Ha'aretz*, 12 June 1998, A1.

19. The Falashmura are a community of Ethiopian Jews who underwent conversion to Christianity, arguably against their will.

20. A great variety of such burial problems are discussed in *Religion and State in Israel* (in Hebrew), ed. Donna Arieli-Horowitz (Jerusalem: Center for Jewish Pluralism of the Movement for Reform Judaism, 1996), 223–31.

21. M. Shalom, "A Jewish Minority in Israel" (in Hebrew), *Hamodi'a*, 12 Sept. 1994. The battle lines over the broadness of the Law of Return are drawn along the secular-religious divide. For an example of a secular position, see Moshe Hanegbi, "The Battle over Immigration" (in Hebrew), *Ma'ariv* (Sabbath

supp.), 1 June 1994; for a religious view, see *Ha'zofeh*, "Danger Is at the Door," 26 May 1994.

22. The number of psulei chitun was not clear until Shitrit came to the Ministry of Religion. It became clear that prior to the immigration from the former Soviet Union the number was in the vicinity of a few hundreds, perhaps even a thousand or so.

23. A description of the various issues in Shitrit's period as minister can be found in Arieli-Horowitz, *Religion and State in Israel*, 240–45.

24. A number of outspoken Orthodox personages make strong cases for civil marriage. See Pinchas Shifman, *Who's Afraid of Civil Marriage?* (in Hebrew) (Jerusalem: Jerusalem Institute for Israel Research, 1995). One of the most sophisticated and influential was the late Ariel Rozen-Tzvi, dean of Tel Aviv University's Law School.

25. Quoted in Lily Galili, "There's No Best Man Yet" (in Hebrew), *Ha'aretz*, 12 July 1998, B2.

26. Quoted ibid.

27. Shachar Ilan, "The Torah Greats Instruct the Initiation of Genealogy Registers in Which Only 'Certain Jews' Will Be Listed" (in Hebrew), *Ha'aretz*, 2 Jan. 1998. See also *Ha'aretz*, 18 Jan. 1998, A6, for follow-up issues.

28. See Avraham Sagi and Tzvi Zohar, *Conversion and Jewish Identity: An Investigation into the Bases of Halacha* (in Hebrew) (Jerusalem: Bialik Institute, Hartman Institute, 1995).

29. Avraham Greenboim, "The Problems in Converting the Immigrants," *Soviet Jews in Transition* (in Hebrew) 2, no. 17 (1995).

30. Pinchas Polansky, "Orthodox Conversion," *Soviet Jews in Transition* (in Hebrew) 2, no. 17 (1995): 260–61.

31. See Eliezer Don Yehiya, *The Politics of Accommodation: Settling Conflicts of State and Religion in Israel* (in Hebrew) (Jerusalem: Florsheimer Institute for Policy Research, 1998).

32. See *The Traditional Movement: History, Principles, Positions, and Challenges* (in Hebrew) (Jerusalem: Traditional Movement, 1994).

33. See *The Reform* (in Hebrew) (Jerusalem: Manof—The Center for Jewish Studies, 1998).

34. Rabbi Lau's remarks were made at a conference held in regard to the Conversion Law and the Ne'eman Commission and published in *Israel and the Diaspora at a Crossroad* (in Hebrew), ed. Shlomo Gur (Jerusalem: Van Leer Institute, 1998), 14–20.

35. Rabbi Ehud Bendel, ibid., 27.

36. See Menahem Friedman, "The Chief Rabbinate: An Irresolvable Dilemma" (in Hebrew), *Medina U'Mimshal Ve'yachasim Beynle'umiyim* 3 (1972): 118–28; and Menahem Friedman, "The Chief Rabbinate as a Religious Leadership: Basic Problems" (in Hebrew), *S'kira Chodshit* (Dec. 1979): 37–44.

37. See, for example, Ran Kislev, "The Lie in the Ne'eman Commission's Compromise" (in Hebrew), *Ha'aretz*, 9 June 1998, B1.

38. Lubotsky spoke at the conference detailed in note 34, quoted in Gur, *Israel and the Diaspora at a Crossroad*, 37.

39. One explosive case of a lenient conversion involved Rabbi Shlomo Goren, who quickly converted Helen Zeidman to avoid a great public fracas over the issue. The Haredim never forgave him for it. See Moshe Zemer, "Rabbi Goren Performs a Reform Conversion" (in Hebrew), in *Sane Halacha* (Tel Aviv: Dvir, 1993), 109–19.

Six   The Future of Consociationalism

1. See Ran Kislev, "This War Has Already Begun" (in Hebrew), *Ha'aretz*, 26 Dec. 1998, B1.

2. See Aviezer Ravitsky, *Is It Really a Kulturkampf?* (in Hebrew) (Jerusalem: Israel Institute for Democracy, 1997); and Eliezer Don Yehiya, *The Politics of Accommodation: Settling Conflicts of State and Religion in Israel* (in Hebrew) (Jerusalem: Florsheimer Institute for Policy Research, 1998).

3. When Israelis are asked to define themselves as Haredi, religious, traditional, or secular, about 25 percent will answer "traditional" and about 50 percent "secular." When, by contrast, they are asked to report on their practices—how much of the Jewish tradition they observe—the numbers are quite different. Traditionalism grows substantially, and secularism shrinks to a far smaller cohort. See the regularly updated figures of the Tami Steinmetz Center for Peace Research, Tel Aviv University, as opposed to the figures presented in *Beliefs, Observances, and Social Interaction among Israeli Jews* (Jerusalem: Louis Guttman Israel Institute for Applied Social Research, 1993).

4. See Charles Liebman and Bernard Susser, "The Forgotten Center: Traditional Jewishness in Israel," *Modern Judaism* 17 (1997): 211–20; and Charles Liebman and Bernard Susser, "Judaism and Jewishness in the Jewish State," *Annals of the American Academy of Political and Social Science* 555 (Jan. 1998): 15–25. Much of the discussion of traditionalism is based on these articles.

Library of Congress Cataloging-in-Publication Data

Cohen, Asher, 1936–
   Israel and the politics of Jewish identity : the secular-
religious impasse / Asher Cohen and Bernard Susser.
   p.   cm.
   Includes bibliographical references and index.
   ISBN 0-8018-6345-7 (alk. paper)
      1. Judaism and state—Israel.   2. Religion and politics—
Israel.   3. Israel—Politics and government.   4. Orthodox
Judaism—Israel—Relations—Nontraditional Jews.
5. Jews—Israel—Identity.   I. Susser, Bernard, 1942–
II. Title.
BM390 .C62 2000
320.95694—dc21   99-089238